FUN GROUP INVOLVING S·K·I·T·S

by Linda Snyder, Tom Tozer, and Amy Nappa

Group

Loveland, Colorado

Fun Group-Involving Skits
Copyright © 1993 Group Publishing, Inc.

CREDITS:

Edited by Mike Nappa

Interior designed by Lisa Smith

Cover designed and illustrated by Bob Fuller and Liz Howe

Except where otherwise noted, scriptures quoted from The Youth Bible, New Century Version, copyright © 1991 by Word Publishing, Dallas, Texas 75039. Used by permission.

Snyder, Linda, 1956–
    Fun group-involving skits / by Linda Snyder, Tom Tozer, and Amy Nappa.
       p.   cm.
    Summary: Includes twenty dramatization activities designed to prompt discussion in youth groups, presenting either specific Bible stories or important topics such as peer pressure, sexuality, or prejudice.
    ISBN 1–55945–152–1
    1. Children's plays, American. 2. Drama in religious education. 3. Christian drama, American. 4. Bible plays, American. [1. Bible plays. 2. Plays. 3. Christian life—Drama.]
    I. Tozer, Tom, 1945– . II. Nappa, Amy, 1963– . III. Title.
PS3569.N893F85 1993
812'.54—dc20   92–41905
                                                     CIP
                                                     AC

12 11 10 9 8 7 6 5   03 02 01 00 99 98 97

Printed in the United States of America.

Contents

Introduction

What's fun, requires no rehearsal, works for any size group, and challenges junior highers to strengthen their relationship with God? A fun group-involving skit, of course!

A group-involving skit is a dramatization activity that gets all members of a junior high group involved, regardless of the size. Because the actors are the audience, everyone's a star during any performance.

This book contains 20 fun skits to bring the Bible to life for junior highers. Each skit deals with either a specific Bible story or a hot issue from a junior higher's life. Each skit also includes help for setting up the show, the script, discussion questions, and ideas for further study of the theme.

Use these innovative skits as creative openers, to spice up the middle of a lesson, or for camp or retreat activities. Your kids will love them because they're fun. You'll love them because of the minimal preparation and powerful impact they can have on your group.

So what are you waiting for? Start using *Fun Group-Involving Skits* today!

SECTION I.
Skits from Scripture

In the Beginning There Was No Tent

What images does the word "creation" bring to mind? A multitude of stars in the sky? A jungle full of wild animals? A sea teeming with underwater life?

How about a circus?

Use this skit to tell the old, old story in a fresh, new way. Introduce your students to the miracle of Creation through the flap of the circus big top. They'll see the Ringmaster at work to create the grandest show of all: life filled with the joy and laughter of knowing God.

Theme:
CREATION

Scripture:
GENESIS 1-2:3
AND PSALM 104

PROPS

For this skit you'll need

- four large sheets of newsprint to represent the circus platforms and pedestals and
- a long strip of yarn to simulate a circus high wire.

SETTING THE STAGE

Before the meeting, read the entire skit at least once to become familiar with the story.

Start the meeting by forming six groups (a group can be one person) and assigning each group the following roles:

Group 1 ....Ringmaster
Group 2 ....Circus calliope (pipe organ)
Group 3 ....Elephants
Group 4 ....Big cats (lions and tigers)
Group 5 ....Chimpanzees
Group 6 ....Clowns

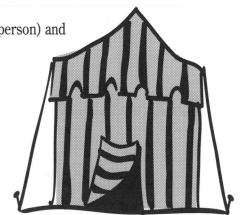

If you have fewer than six group members, have kids act out more than one role. Give groups a few minutes to decide on actions that will represent their characters.

Say: **I'll be reading the skit** *In the Beginning There Was No Tent.* **Each time I pause, you'll have up to 15 seconds to come up with** pantomime actions that illustrate the skit. Sometimes only one group's character will be called on to perform; other times everyone will be involved. You'll need to pay attention to what's going on during the skit. But before we begin, let's practice one pantomime we'll all use in this skit—the construction of a tent.

Have kids form a circle and hold hands. Teach the group how to construct a tent by raising their clasped hands as they step toward the center of the circle. Practice two or three times before starting the skit.

After a few trial runs at making a tent, re-form the circle. Read the skit enthusiastically and encourage everyone to ham it up when it comes their time to perform.

THE PERFORMANCE:
In the Beginning There Was No Tent

In the beginning, there was nothing, nada, zilch. And the Ringmaster said, "Let there be a tent!" *(Pause for Ringmaster's actions)* And there was a tent. *(Pause for entire group's actions)* And the Ringmaster said, "It's good!" *(Pause for Ringmaster's actions)*

And there was a red and white striped tent upon the earth the first day. *(Pause for entire group's actions)*

Then the Ringmaster listened, listened for melodious sound *(Pause for Ringmaster's actions)* but there was no sound at all.

And the Ringmaster said, "Let there be sound!" *(Pause for Ringmaster's actions)* And there was a calliope. *(Pause for calliope's actions)* And the Ringmaster played the keys, *(Pause for Ringmaster's actions)* and the calliope tooted high sounds and low sounds, *(Pause for calliope's actions)* long sounds and short sounds, *(Pause for calliope's actions)* happy sounds and sad sounds. *(Pause for calliope's actions)* And the Ringmaster danced while the calliope played. *(Pause for Ringmaster's and calliope's actions)* The Ringmaster laughed and said, "It's good!" *(Pause for Ringmaster's actions)*

And there was a calliope *(Pause for calliope's actions)* inside the tent the second day. *(Pause for entire group's actions)*

But the Ringmaster wasn't finished yet. The Ringmaster said, "Let there be strong, large, awesome creatures to fill up my tent!" *(Pause for Ringmaster's actions)* And it was so. And the Ringmaster called them "elephants." *(Pause for elephants' actions)*

The elephants stomped their feet, *(Pause for elephants' actions)* swung their trunks, *(Pause for elephants' actions)* stood end to end on hind legs, *(Pause for elephants' actions)* and twirled their massive bodies in circles on tiny platforms. *(Pause, and place the sheets of newsprint on the ground for elephants' actions. Make sure kids are aware the newsprint represents the platforms.)* And the tent was filled with the mighty sound of elephants' trumpeting. *(Pause for elephants' actions)* And the Ringmaster said, "It's good!" *(Pause for Ringmaster's actions)*

And there were elephants *(Pause for elephants' actions)* inside the tent the third day. *(Pause for entire group's actions)*

The Ringmaster was really beginning to enjoy himself, so he said, "Let there be animals of unusual courage and cunning!" *(Pause for Ringmaster's actions)* And the big cats came into being. *(Pause for big cats' actions)* The Ringmaster called them "lions" and "tigers."

They were sleek and swift *(Pause for big cats' actions)* and ferocious. *(Pause for big cats' actions)* The lions showed off their great crowns of magnificent hair about their heads. *(Pause for big cats' actions)* The tigers showed off their awesome stripes of regal beauty. *(Pause for big cats' actions)*

The Ringmaster tamed the fierce creatures. *(Pause for Ringmaster's and big cats' actions)* On command, they performed tricks for the Ringmaster, jumping from pedestal to pedestal. *(Pause for big cats' actions. Tell big cats to use the newsprint as pedestals.)* They roared and they snarled, *(Pause for big cats' actions)* but they always obeyed. *(Pause for Ringmaster's and big cats' actions)* And the Ringmaster saw that it was good. *(Pause for Ringmaster's actions)*

And there were big cats *(Pause for big cats' actions)* in the tent the fourth day. *(Pause for Ringmaster's actions)*

The Ringmaster looked for more excitement but could find none. *(Pause for Ringmaster's actions)* So the Ringmaster said, "Let there be great feats of balancing and daring in my tent!" *(Pause for Ringmaster's actions)* And the Ringmaster made a high wire. *(Pause, place the yarn on the floor, and tell kids to use it as the high wire.)* On the wire the Ringmaster created chimpanzees. *(Pause for chimpanzees' actions)*

The chimpanzees did flips and turns and acrobatic wonders. *(Pause for chimpanzees' actions)* They rode bicycles on the high wire. *(Pause for chimpanzees' actions)* They swung through the air—back and forth, back and forth. *(Pause for chimpanzees' actions)* And sometimes they fell into the great net that the loving Ringmaster had provided. *(Pause for chimpanzees' actions)* And the Ringmaster saw that it was good. *(Pause for Ringmaster's actions)*

And there were chimpanzees *(Pause for chimpanzees' actions)* in the tent the fifth day. *(Pause for entire group's actions)*

There was the beauty of the tent, *(Pause for entire group's actions)* the melody of the calliope, *(Pause for calliope's actions)* the trumpeting of the elephants, *(Pause for elephants' actions)* the tricks of the big cats, *(Pause for big cats' actions)* and the excitement of the chimpanzees on the high wire. *(Pause for chimpanzees' actions)*

And still, the Ringmaster was not satisfied. So the Ringmaster said, "Let me make clowns in my image, in my likeness, and let them rule over the circus." *(Pause for Ringmaster's actions)*

The Ringmaster laughed *(Pause for Ringmaster's actions)* and in the laughter created clowns. *(Pause for clowns' actions)* They were the image of the Ringmaster, with funny eyes to see hurts, *(Pause for clowns' actions)* great ears to listen, *(Pause for clowns' actions)* big, red noses to sniff out the good in everyone, *(Pause for clowns' actions)* strong arms to carry each other,

(Pause for clowns' actions) and wide smiles to share the Ringmaster's message of love, peace, and laughter. *(Pause for clowns' actions)*

And the Ringmaster blessed the clowns and said to them, "Laugh and make others laugh with you. Share my love and take care of all the other creatures of the circus." *(Pause for Ringmaster's actions)* And it was so. The Ringmaster saw all that had been made, and it was very good. *(Pause for Ringmaster's actions)*

And there were clowns and laughter *(Pause for clowns' actions)* in the tent the sixth day. *(Pause for entire group's actions)*

Thus the circus was completed with all its memories and magnificence. So on the seventh day, the Ringmaster and all his creatures rested from the work. *(Pause for entire group's actions)* And the Ringmaster blessed the seventh day and made it holy. *(Pause for Ringmaster's actions)*

And the Greatest Show on Earth continues to this day under the tent of love and guidance made by the Ringmaster-Creator.

(Pause, then lead the group in a round of applause for everyone's performances.)

BEFORE THE FINAL CURTAIN

Have kids read Genesis 1:1–2:3 and Psalm 104 and discuss these questions.
1. In what ways are Genesis 1–2:3, Psalm 104, and the story of the circus alike?
2. How do you feel when you think about God's creative work? How are you a part of God's creative work?
3. What responsibilities do we have toward God's "tent," the world? toward God's "clowns," each other?

AFTER THE SHOW

Try these activities for further study.
1. Have each student make a sculpture out of modeling clay that represents him or her. Next, have group members each list on paper 10 ways they're created in God's image and place the list next to their sculpture. Encourage kids to share their sculptures and lists with the rest of the group. Allow group members to tell additional ways they see God in one another.
2. Form two groups. Give each group a stack of magazines, old posters, newspapers, glue, and newsprint. Using their supplies, have one group design a collage of the world as God created it to be. Have the other

group make a collage of how the world is today. Afterward, have groups compare their worlds. Hang them in your meeting room as a reminder that we're called to care for—not trash—the world.

It Happened One Century

For many junior highers, Bible history can be boring. But the history of Noah and the great flood carries with it a message of hope and faithfulness kids need to hear.

Use this skit to help youth group members experience the story of Noah and the flood in a new and exciting way. As they act out their parts in this modernized version of the biblical account, they'll gain a new appreciation for the history of God's faithfulness recorded in the scriptures.

Theme:
THE GREAT FLOOD

Scripture:
GENESIS 6:5–8:22

PROPS

No supplies are needed for this skit.

SETTING THE STAGE

Before the meeting, read the entire skit at least once to become familiar with the story.

At the meeting, form pairs and teach kids the following cue words and actions:

Cue Word	Actions
NOAH	Partners dance in circles and shout, "I'm singin' in the rain."
GOD	Raise hands and shout "Awesome!"
PEOPLE	Partners give each other a high five and say, "Let's party!"
FLOOD	Entire group performs a "wave." (Starting with students on the left side of the room, kids stand, raise arms, and sit back down again in rapid succession.)
ANIMALS	Pairs imitate an animal of their choice.
RAIN or WATER	Hold nose and say, "Glub, glub, glub!"
DOVE	Flap arms and say, "Olive, anyone?"

Have students practice the actions at least once before the performance. Then read the skit aloud, pausing for actions each time you read an italicized word. Be sure to allow enough time for kids to complete their actions before moving ahead with the story.

THE PERFORMANCE:
It Happened One Century

This is the story of *NOAH* and the *FLOOD*.

NOAH was a good man. He always brushed his teeth and fed his dog table scraps. But most importantly, he followed *GOD* faithfully.

Other *PEOPLE* on earth were rotten. They didn't care a bit about what *GOD* said. All the *PEOPLE* wanted to do was have a good time. The result was high crime, general evil-doing, and dumb cartoons on Saturday mornings.

When *GOD* saw that everyone on the earth did evil, *GOD* said, "*NOAH*, we have a problem. *PEOPLE* have made my earth full of violence, evil-doing, and dumb cartoons. So, I've decided to wipe *PEOPLE* from the face of the earth. But I'd like to keep you around for awhile.

"I'm going to bring a *FLOOD* of *WATER* on earth to destroy all living things—*ANIMALS* , *PEOPLE*, everything. Except you and your family, of course. *NOAH*, I want you to build a little boat to escape the *RAIN*. Better make that a big boat—you're going to have some company.

"Bring into the boat two of every living *ANIMAL*, one male and one female. It'll be nice to have some *ANIMALS* around after the *FLOOD*. Unless you don't like snakes. Then it could be kind of a bummer. But, hey, that's life in the *ANIMAL* kingdom.

Gather some food and store it on the boat. But don't worry about drinks—there'll be plenty of *WATER*.

After he recovered from fainting, *NOAH* did everything *GOD* commanded of him. *NOAH* and his family made a big boat and went into the boat to escape the *WATERS* of the *FLOOD*.

The *FLOOD* started when *NOAH* was 600 years old. *RAIN* fell on earth for 40 days and 40 nights. *WATER* flooded everything. The first thing to go under *WATER* was the television station that aired the dumb cartoons. After that, whole cities of *PEOPLE* were drowned. At first, *PEOPLE* thought it was just another pool party. Then a few *PEOPLE* figured out what was really happening, but it was too late.

The *WATER* rose so much that even the highest mountains under the sky were covered by it. Before long, all the *ANIMALS* and *PEOPLE* on the earth had been destroyed. All that was left was *NOAH*, the *ANIMALS* in the boat, and *NOAH'S* family. The *WATER* continued to cover the earth for 150 days. And the boat smelled a lot like wet *ANIMALS*. But *GOD* remembered *NOAH*, the *ANIMALS* in the boat, and *NOAH'S* family. *GOD* made a wind blow over the earth, and the *WATER* went down.

NOAH opened a window he had made in the boat, and he sent out a raven. The raven never came back. (Ravens have never traveled by boat since.) Then *NOAH* sent out a *DOVE* to see if the *WATER* had dried up. When at last the *DOVE* brought *NOAH* an olive leaf, *NOAH* knew it would soon be safe to leave the boat.

GOD made a covenant with *NOAH*. *GOD* said he would never again destroy all living things by a *FLOOD*. And *GOD* put a rainbow in the sky as a sign of his covenant with *NOAH*.

And that's the story of *NOAH* and the *FLOOD*.

BEFORE THE FINAL CURTAIN

Have pairs read the actual account of the great flood in Genesis 6:5–8:22 and discuss these questions.
1. How do you feel when you hear the story of Noah and the flood? How would you feel if the flood had happened in this century?
2. Who do you relate to most in this story? Why?
3. The rainbow is a sign of hope for Noah and for us. What are other signs of hope for you? Explain.

AFTER THE SHOW

Try these activities for further study.
1. Form two groups and give each group a copy of the same newspaper. Have one group look for evidence of evil in the world while the other group looks for evidence of hope in the world. Have groups share their discoveries and discuss ways they can spread God's hope to their world.
2. Have students create a large rainbow mural for your meeting room wall. Inside the colors of the rainbow, have kids write promises of hope God has made to us.

And the Walls Came Tumbling Down

Theme:

THE BATTLE OF JERICHO

Scripture:

JOSHUA 1:3-9 AND 6

*C*ould he do it? Was he scared? Could Joshua really overcome the walls of Jericho?

We all know that Joshua not only could do it, but he did do it. With God as his strategist and providing the muscle, Joshua and his men plowed through a seemingly insurmountable obstacle. Sweet victory came as a result of their obedience to God.

How about your group members? Can they do it? Are they scared to follow God through the obstacles of life? Use this skit to encourage them to trust God and plow forward in obedience to God's Word.

PROPS

No props are needed for this skit.

SETTING THE STAGE

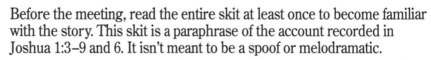

Before the meeting, read the entire skit at least once to become familiar with the story. This skit is a paraphrase of the account recorded in Joshua 1:3–9 and 6. It isn't meant to be a spoof or melodramatic.

Say: **Not long after being freed from slavery in Egypt, Joshua and the Israelites took a great risk in attacking the city of Jericho. This walled city seemed an impossible obstacle for a bunch of ex-slaves to try to conquer. Yet they trusted in God, and conquer it they did.**

Let's see if we can re-create some of the tension and excitement of this story from history by performing the skit *And the Walls Came Tumbling Down.*

Form a circle and have kids number off from one to four. Teach kids the following cue words and actions:

Cue Word	Actions
JOSHUA	Ones, salute and stand at attention.
TRUMPETS	Twos, form fake trumpets with your fists and make a loud trumpeting sound.

QUIET	Threes, put your fingers on your lips and say "SHHH."
BATTLE	Fours, stamp your feet and fake boxing an opponent.
JERICHO	Everyone, put your hands at your side and move toward the center of the circle until you've formed a human wall.
MARCH	Everyone, turn to the right and march around in a circle to the count of "Hup, Two, Three, Four!"

Have kids quickly practice responses to the cue words, then begin the performance.

THE PERFORMANCE:
And the Walls Came Tumbling Down

It all started long, long ago. Moses died, and *JOSHUA* was left to lead the Israelites into their new territory.

The Lord spoke to *JOSHUA* and said, "I will give you every place you go in the land of Canaan. *JOSHUA*, be strong and brave! Always remember my words, written down by Moses. Don't be afraid, because the Lord your God will be with you everywhere you go."

And so it began—*JOSHUA* and the *BATTLE* of *JERICHO*.

JERICHO stood at the entrance to the promised land of Canaan. Great, thick walls surrounded the city, protecting it from invasion. *JOSHUA* knew the king of *JERICHO* feared him, and yet the walls seemed an impossible obstacle to overcome.

But God had plans to overcome, and he told *JOSHUA* his unusual strategy: *MARCH* around the city, blow the *TRUMPETS*, and the walls will come tumbling down.

JOSHUA wondered at God's strange *BATTLE* orders. But *JOSHUA* trusted God completely and knew that *JERICHO* would be his for the taking.

The people of *JERICHO* were afraid. They closed the city gates and guarded the great walls. No one came in, and no one went out.

It was time for the *BATTLE* to begin, and the Israelites were amazed at what happened next. Instead of calling the brave, young soldiers, *JOSHUA* called the priests forward. "Seven of you," *JOSHUA* said, "take your *TRUMPETS* and *MARCH* at the front of the procession. The rest of you follow, carrying the Ark from God's tent, as a sign that God himself is with us."

Next, *JOSHUA* placed some soldiers in front of the Ark and some soldiers behind the Ark. *JOSHUA* said nothing about a *BATTLE*, nothing about the walls, nothing about weapons. When everyone was lined up, *JOSHUA* gave his next instructions just as God had given them to him.

"*MARCH* around *JERICHO*, blowing your *TRUMPETS* as you go. Soldiers, keep *QUIET* and don't yell a *BATTLE* cry. Now *MARCH* around the city walls one time and then come back to camp. That'll be all for today."

The king of *JERICHO* looked down over the wall and saw the huge crowd assembled. When he heard the first blast of *TRUMPETS*, he thought the *BATTLE* had begun. But tooting *TRUMPETS* was the only action taken by the army. The king of *JERICHO* watched as the *QUIET* group *MARCHED* one time around the walls.

Early the next morning, it was the same story. The priests carried the Ark of the Lord and their *TRUMPETS*. The priests blew their *TRUMPETS* without ceasing. Soldiers *MARCHED* in front of and behind the Ark of the Lord. All was *QUIET*, except for the sound of *TRUMPETS*. Once around *JERICHO* they marched.

For six days in a row it was the same: priests carrying the Ark, *QUIET* soldiers, *TRUMPETS* blaring, once around the city walls, and *QUIETLY* back to camp. The people of *JERICHO* watched and waited, growing more afraid each day.

On the seventh day, *JOSHUA* had new orders for the Israelites. "*MARCH* around *JERICHO* seven times," he said. "The first six times be absolutely *QUIET*. The seventh time around, blow the *TRUMPETS* and shout a loud *BATTLE* cry, for today, the Lord will give you the city of *JERICHO*."

And so, lap one, they *MARCHED QUIETLY*. Two, three, four, five, six times the soldiers and priests *MARCHED* around the walls *QUIETLY*. Then on the seventh lap, above the shrill *TRUMPET* sound, the mighty *BATTLE* cry of the Israelite soldiers was heard. They shouted as if their lungs would burst.

At that very moment, the great, thick, impenetrable walls trembled. And shook. And came tumbling down. With cries of triumph and excitement, God's people defeated the city of *JERICHO* with its great walls.

The walls came tumbling down because *JOSHUA* trusted God and didn't rely on his own strength or *BATTLE* tactics. The Lord was with *JOSHUA*, and *JOSHUA* was famous throughout the land. (Paraphrased from Joshua 6)

BEFORE THE FINAL CURTAIN

Have kids sit down in the circle, read Joshua 6, and discuss these questions.

1. How did you feel as you fought the battle of Jericho? How do you think the cast of characters felt as it was actually happening back then? The soldiers? The priests? The Israelite people? Joshua?

2. Do you think Joshua ever doubted they would win? Why or why not? Do you ever doubt God's power in the world today? Why or why not?

3. What part did faith play in the battle of Jericho? What part does faith play in your life today? Be specific.

4. What obstacles do you face that seem as awesome as the walls of Jericho? How can God help you overcome them?

AFTER THE SHOW

Try these activities for further study.

1. Form two to four groups. Give each group several sheets of newsprint, a thick-tipped magic marker, and masking tape. At the signal, challenge your kids to write down obstacles to living a Christian life in today's world. Have them write one obstacle per sheet of newsprint (in large lettering) and tape each sheet on a wall.

When all groups are finished, have kids take turns reading the newsprint and telling why they chose the obstacles they did. Then have kids answer this question: **How can the story of the battle of Jericho help us overcome the obstacles we wrote on these walls?**

2. Take your group on an ice cream adventure. Go to a nearby ice cream parlor and either treat kids to or have kids buy a scoop. However, place this one condition on their purchase: They can only choose a flavor of ice cream they've never tried before. Then let kids enjoy their treats.

Afterward ask:

- **How did you feel when you were deciding which flavor you'd buy?**
- **How did you arrive at your final decision?**
- **How was the risk involved in choosing an ice cream flavor like the risk involved in acting in faith on God's promises?**
- **How can you act in faith on God's promises this week? this month? this year?**

Dave and the Gorillas

Theme:

DAVID AND GOLIATH

Scripture:

1 SAMUEL 17

The story of David and Goliath is about a kid and a giant, right? Wrong! It's a story about faith and doing the impossible. It's an historical account of a boy who put his faith into action and, despite the odds, conquered a feared foe.

Junior highers today struggle to overcome the "giants" that challenge their faith. They often feel weak in the face of peer pressure and societal standards. Use this skit to help kids realize that the same God who gave David victory over Goliath is only a prayer away. When junior highers turn to God in prayer and place their faith in him, they too, can slay giants.

PROPS

No props are needed for this skit.

SETTING THE STAGE

Before the meeting, read the entire skit at least once to become familiar with the story.

Form four groups. Use half the class to form group 1 and the rest of the class to form groups 2, 3, and 4. Assign groups the following roles:

Group 1	Garth's Gorillas
Group 2	Dave's Daredevils
Group 3	Innocent Bystanders
Group 4	Troubled Teachers

If you have fewer than five group members, have kids act out more than one role.

Then say: **I'll be reading the skit** *Dave and the Gorillas,* **which is a modern version of the story of David and Goliath. When I pause during the skit, that'll be your cue to act out your group's part. For example, if I say, "Garth's Gorillas growled at Dave's Daredevils," and pause, then the Gorillas group should growl at the Daredevils group. Be creative and have fun with this.**

One last disclaimer: The characters in this story are imaginary. Any similarity to anyone you know personally is purely coincidental. Ready? Let's begin.

Read the skit enthusiastically and encourage everyone to ham it up when it comes their time to perform.

THE PERFORMANCE:
Dave and the Gorillas

Every school has a bully. Jefferson High had a bunch of them. And Garth's Gorillas were the worst Jefferson High had ever seen.

Garth's Gorillas were a mess—a mean mess—and their tempers were nasty. When they got mad, they waved their smelly sneakers in front of the nearest Innocent Bystander, making the Bystander pass out. *(Pause for Garth's Gorillas' and Innocent Bystanders' actions)* When they were feeling kind, they simply growled at Dave's Daredevils. *(Pause for Garth's Gorillas' actions)*

Because the Gorillas had no manners, the Troubled Teachers just got used to hearing the Gorillas burp during their lectures. *(Pause for Troubled Teachers' and Garth's Gorillas' actions)* Because the Gorillas refused to shower, the Innocent Bystanders and Dave's Daredevils simply got used to holding their noses all day long. *(Pause for Innocent Bystanders' and Dave's Daredevils' actions)* No one liked Garth's Gorillas, and everyone was afraid of them.

Anyway, on one fateful Monday morning, the bell rang at eight o'clock sharp.

The Gorillas said, "Kiss our feet!" *(Pause for Garth's Gorillas' actions)* And the Troubled Teachers pretended to kiss them. *(Pause for Troubled Teachers' actions)* Twice, as usual. *(Pause for Troubled Teachers' actions)*

The Gorillas said, "Do our homework!" *(Pause for Garth's Gorillas' actions)* And Dave's Daredevils jogged over to ace each assignment. *(Pause for Dave's Daredevils' actions)*

The Gorillas said, "Give us your lunch money!" *(Pause for Garth's Gorillas' actions)* And the Innocent Bystanders emptied their pockets. *(Pause for Innocent Bystanders' actions)*

And there you have it. Jefferson High on a normal Monday morning.

The principal called his army of Troubled Teachers to deal with Garth's Gorillas. He said, "Stop those kids! Act like grownups!"

But the Troubled Teachers just trembled and shook with fear. *(Pause for Troubled Teachers' actions)* They cried, "They'll stuff us in their lockers! Get someone else to do it!" They turned their backs on the problem of Garth's Gorillas and hoped it would go away by itself. *(Pause for Troubled Teachers' actions)*

The Innocent Bystanders were summoned. They chewed their fingernails, *(Pause for Innocent Bystanders' actions)* bit their lips, *(Pause for Innocent Bystanders' actions)* and searched the encyclopedia for a solution. *(Pause for Innocent Bystanders' actions)* But "bully" wasn't listed. Shaking their heads, *(Pause for Innocent Bystanders' actions)* they shuffled their feet out of the principal's office, heads held low in shame. *(Pause for Innocent Bystanders' actions)*

No one could stop Garth's Gorillas. And it was going to get worse. Next week, Jefferson High would be humiliated at the All Star Gymnastics Tournament because Garth's Gorillas had decided they were going to represent the school at the tournament.

The Gorillas practiced their jumps. *(Pause for Garth's Gorillas' actions)* And fell flat on their faces. *(Pause for Garth's Gorillas' actions)* They tried to walk on the balance beam. *(Pause for Garth's Gorillas' actions)* And tripped on their shoelaces. *(Pause for Garth's Gorillas' actions)*

But when the Innocent Bystanders, the Troubled Teachers, and Dave's Daredevils laughed, *(Pause for Innocent Bystanders', Dave's Daredevils', and Troubled Teachers' actions)* the Gorillas beat their chests in anger *(Pause for Garth's Gorillas' actions)* and shouted, "Cowards, all of you! We're the strongest and best at everything! We dare anyone to compete with our team! How about it, you Innocent Bystanders? Any of you have the guts?"

The Innocent Bystanders simply fainted. *(Pause for Innocent Bystanders' actions)* Actually, they were only pretending to faint, but their ploy worked. The Gorillas forgot about them.

"How about you, Troubled Teachers," bellowed Garth's Gorillas. "Or are you all chicken?"

The Troubled Teachers thought about it, then did their best imitations of barnyard hens. *(Pause for Troubled Teachers' actions)*

The Gorillas laughed. *(Pause for Garth's Gorillas' actions)* One of them said, "I'll bet none of you chess-playin', homework-doin', God-followin', Bible-readin', cross-carryin' sissy Daredevils would dare challenge us either." They laughed some more. *(Pause for Garth's Gorillas' actions)*

Suddenly, something snapped in Dave's Daredevils' hearts. The Gorillas could mock chess or make light of homework, but nobody could make fun of God.

The Daredevils stepped forward *(Pause for Dave's Daredevils' actions)* and said, "Come on, Gorillas, make our day." *(Pause for Dave's Daredevils' actions)*

Garth's Gorillas started laughing even louder. *(Pause for Garth's Gorillas' actions)* They formed a circle around the Daredevils *(Pause for Garth's Gorillas' actions)* and said, "Now what're you gonna do, Bible Bums?" *(Pause for Garth's Gorillas' actions)*

Silence echoed throughout the school. Then Dave's Daredevils said simply, "Pray." *(Pause for Dave's Daredevils' actions)*

The Daredevils knelt to pray. *(Pause for Dave's Daredevils' actions)* Garth's Gorillas were stunned. They scratched their heads in confusion. *(Pause for Garth's Gorillas' actions)* Quietly, ever so quietly, the Innocent Bystanders and the Troubled Teachers started whispering, "Go, Daredevils, go." *(Pause for Innocent Bystanders' and Troubled Teachers' actions)*

Garth's Gorillas shielded their eyes because the Daredevils started glowing. *(Pause for Garth's Gorillas' actions)* Still, the Daredevils prayed. And the Innocent Bystanders and the Troubled Teachers chanted just a little louder, "Go, Daredevils, go." *(Pause for Innocent Bystanders' and Troubled Teachers' actions)*

Suddenly, Dave's Daredevils stood *(Pause for Dave's Daredevils' actions)* and shouted, "Victory is the Lord's!" *(Pause for Dave's Daredevils' actions)* One by one, they blew a short puff of air on each Gorilla. *(Pause for Dave's Daredevils' actions)* The stunned Gorillas fell unconscious, utterly defeated. *(Pause for Garth's Gorillas' actions)*

The school erupted with cheers and shouts. *(Pause for Innocent Bystanders', the Troubled Teachers', and Dave's Daredevils' actions)* Then Dave's Daredevils told everyone to be quiet. *(Pause for Dave's Daredevils' actions)*

"Let's give credit where credit is due," they said. "Let's all pray." *(Pause for Dave's Daredevils' actions)*

So the Daredevils, the Innocent Bystanders, the Troubled Teachers, and yes, even Garth's Gorillas, knelt to pray. *(Pause for Innocent Bystanders', Dave's Daredevils', Troubled Teachers' and Garth's Gorillas' actions)*

(Leader—As your group is kneeling, pray this simple prayer: **Lord, thank you for giving us the power to overcome anyone who would oppose our faith in you. Help us to rely on your power more each day. Remind us of the weapon we have in prayer and help us to turn our prayers into reality by trusting in you. In Jesus' name, amen.)**

BEFORE THE FINAL CURTAIN

Have groups read the story of David and Goliath in 1 Samuel 17 and discuss these questions.

1. How did you feel during this skit? Why? How do you think David and the Israelites felt when faced with Goliath? Why?
2. What "gorillas," or obstacles, stand in your way as you try to live a fulfilling, Christian life? How can you overcome them?
3. What part did faith play in the Bible story and skit? What role does faith play in your life? How can we increase our faith?

AFTER THE SHOW

Try these activities for further study.

1. Sponsor a prayer-fest at your church. Have kids poll other church members to find out prayer needs in the congregation. Then have kids spend an evening at the church praying for the needs of these people. Have kids sign up to be responsible to pray for 15-minute intervals. Set up an altar kids can kneel at as they pray.

After the prayer-fest is over, celebrate with some snacks.

2. Have kids brainstorm a list of everything they did on a particular day that required a measure of faith; for example, sitting in a chair, eating cafeteria food, or driving to church. After kids have each completed their list, have them make a new list of things in life that require faith in God. Kids might list things like eternal life, facing temptation, and believing the Bible. Have kids compare the two lists and discuss ways to increase their faith in God.

Cookin' Good

Many young people are willing to take a stand for their faith but just don't know how. Others cave in at the slightest opposition and then feel guilty about it afterward. Use this echo-pantomime about Shadrach, Meshach, and Abednego to encourage your kids as they struggle to stand up for what they believe.

Theme:
THE FIERY FURNACE

Scripture:
DANIEL 1:1-21 AND 3:1-30

PROPS

For this skit you'll need

- a copy of the performance section of the skit.

SETTING THE STAGE

Before the meeting, read the entire skit at least once to become familiar with the story. Also, select one volunteer to lead the pantomime actions and give him or her a copy of the performance section of the skit. Have your volunteer read the skit beforehand and practice the pantomime actions.

At the meeting, have the group stand, facing you and your volunteer. Inform kids they will be experiencing an echo-pantomime based on the story of Shadrach, Meshach, and Abednego. Tell students to act out what you say by mimicking the pantomime actions of the volunteer. Then begin reading the skit.

THE PERFORMANCE: *Cookin' Good*

The Script	The Actions
King Nebuchadnezzar won the war.	Thumbs down
God's people were defeated.	Pretend to slit your throat

The Script	The Actions
Shadrach, Meshach, and Abednego were taken captive	Cross outstretched arms and clench fists as if in shackles
to serve the king.	Kneel on one knee and bow down
Nasty!	Put finger in open mouth and gag
The king gave Shadrach, Meshach, and Abednego a certain amount of food and wine every day—	Make eating motions
food that was forbidden by God	Shake finger back and forth
and was nasty!	Put finger in open mouth and gag
The young men refused to eat.	Hold both hands over mouth
The king's chief officer was scared.	Bite nails on both hands
He said, "You'll get weak and thin.	Suck in gut
Then the king will chop off my head!"	Hold neck tightly and stick out tongue
For ten days	Hold up ten fingers
they ate kosher food,	Applaud
and they grew	Squat and stand up
healthier than the king's men.	Rub stomach and smile
God's team won	Thumbs up
that food fight.	Make eating motions, then shake fists
God gave Shadrach, Meshach, and Abednego	Outstretch arms
special wisdom,	Point to head
and they honored and loved God.	Hug yourself
Time passed.	Make sweeping motion with one arm

The Script	The Actions
The king forgot	Scratch head
about God.	Raise hands in praise
He built a huge, gold statue	Put hand over eyes (like a visor) and look up
and ordered the people	Point one finger and shake it at the group
to bow down and worship it.	Fold hands and bow down
The king said, "If you say no,	Make an X with two fingers and shake head no
I'll throw you in the fiery furnace."	Wipe brow and fan face furiously
The music played.	Pretend to play a flute
Everyone bowed low.	Bow down
Shadrach, Meshach, and Abednego stood tall	Raise both arms high
and looked at the sky.	Put hands over eyes (like a visor) and look up
The king was mad	Shake clenched fist
and gave an order.	Point one finger and shake it at the group
"Uh-oh," said the king.	Cup cheeks in hands and open eyes wide
"Throw them in the furnace!"	Wipe brow and fan face furiously
The three guys	Hold up three fingers
told the king their God could save them.	Raise both hands in praise gesture
But even if he didn't,	Shrug shoulders and hold out hands to the side
they wouldn't bow down	Make an X with two fingers and shake head no
and worship the idol	Fold hands in prayer
of the king.	Cup hands on top of head to form a crown
The fire was seven times	Hold up seven fingers

The Script	The Actions
hotter than usual	Wipe brow and fan face furiously
when Shadrach, Meshach, and Abednego entered.	Outstretch arms
Three men in the fire,	Hold up three fingers
and when the king looked,	Pretend to hold up binoculars
he couldn't believe	Shake head no
what he saw.	Point to eyes
Four men in the fire now—	Hold up four fingers
one looked like a god,	Hold up one finger and then raise arms in praise
and none of them burned—	Applaud
Wow!	Raise left fist high and then raise right fist
The king pulled them out.	Pretend to pull a Tug-of-War rope
Not a hair was burned!	Pull hair on your head
The three didn't even smell like smoke.	Hold nose and shake head no
Praise God!	Applaud
The king bowed low	Bow down
and said, "Your God must be real.	Hold two thumbs up
He saved you from certain death."	Pretend to slit your throat
And the king decreed	Hit two clenched fists together
that all should honor	Raise hands in praise
the God of the three brave men.	Hold up three fingers
So-o-o,	Make sweeping motion with one arm
trust in God	Put hand over heart
and don't bow down	Make an X with pointer fingers and shake head no

The Script	The Actions
to the false gods in the world today.	Hold up two thumbs down
There's only one God	Hold up one finger
who can truly save,	Outstretch arms to form a cross
as shown by	Pretend to hold up binoculars
three men in a furnace	Hold up three fingers
who were really brave.	Hold arms out to the side and flex muscles

BEFORE THE FINAL CURTAIN

Have kids form trios and read Daniel 1:1-21 and 3:1-30. Then have them discuss these questions.

1. How were Shadrach, Meshach, and Abednego pressured to compromise their faith? How are you pressured to compromise your faith?
2. Shadrach, Meshach, and Abednego's society worshiped the golden image of the king. What things, such as money or fame, does our society worship?
3. How do you respond to people who don't respect your beliefs?
4. How would you feel about God if Shadrach, Meshach, and Abednego had been consumed by the fire? Explain. How do you feel knowing God allows people to die for their faith today? Explain.

AFTER THE SHOW

Try these activities for further study.

1. Devise a "Just Follow Your Beliefs" campaign. Form groups of no more than four and have them come up with a list of options students have when confronted with people who oppose their faith. Have each foursome share its list with the entire group. Then, as a group, select the top 10 ideas. Have kids write these on a 3×5 card to take home as a reminder of how to face opposition to their faith.
2. In groups of no more than six (a group can be one person), have students create modern-day skits of Shadrach, Meshach, and Abednego. Spark kids' creativity by asking: **What if Shadrach, Meshach, and Abednego went to your school? were members of our church? were sports stars?**

Then have groups perform their skits for everyone in the meeting.

The Tale of the Whale

Theme:

JONAH AND
THE BIG FISH

Scripture:

JONAH 1–4

*T*hree days in the belly of a big fish. That's what it took for the runaway prophet Jonah to learn the importance of obeying an all-powerful God. Then, through Jonah's obedience, the people of Nineveh experienced the power of God's forgiving love.

Junior highers today aren't likely to be swallowed by a big fish, but like Jonah, they often try to run from God and his forgiveness. Use this skit to help your youth group members experience firsthand the power behind God's forgiving love.

PROPS

No props are needed for this skit.

SETTING THE STAGE

Before the meeting, read the entire skit at least once to become familiar with the story.

Form five groups and assign each group one of the following roles:

Group 1	Jonah
Group 2	Sailors
Group 3	Wind and sea
Group 4	Big fish
Group 5	People of Nineveh

With the exception of group 2, a group can be one person. Group 2 should be at least two people. If you have fewer than six students, have groups play more than one role.

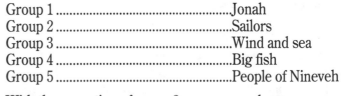

Instruct groups to get in the following positions to start the skit:

JONAH	Lie down as if you're in bed.
SAILORS	Sit single file, in a row, facing the same direction, as if lined up in a canoe.
WIND AND SEA	Form a circle and hook arms.
BIG FISH	Lie on the floor and imitate a fish.
PEOPLE OF NINEVEH	Sit in a circle and pretend to play with dice.

Say: **Today we're going to bring the story of Jonah and the big fish to life. I'll read a paraphrase of Jonah, chapters 1 through 4. As I read, your group will perform actions that correspond to what your role is doing in the narrative. Remember to perform as a group and to respond to what you hear in the story. When I pause, that'll be your cue to begin acting. Let's have fun with this!**

Read dramatically and urge kids to act out their parts enthusiastically. Especially encourage the kids playing nonhuman roles to be creative in their performances. Much of the fun in this skit will be a result of their creativity.

THE PERFORMANCE:
The Tale of the Whale

One day, God spoke to Jonah and said, "Get up, go to the great city of Nineveh, and preach against it, because I see the evil things they do."

Jonah got up all right—on the wrong side of his bed, and he ran away from God. *(Pause for Jonah's actions)*

Jonah ran to the city of Joppa, where he found sailors going in the opposite direction of Nineveh. *(Pause for Jonah's and sailors' actions)*

Jonah paid the sailors for his passage *(Pause for Jonah's and sailors' actions)* and climbed aboard their boat, planning to run further away from God.

But God sent a great storm of wind and sea upon the sailors *(Pause for wind and sea's and sailors' actions)*, which caused so much havoc that the ship was in danger of breaking apart.

The wind blew, *(Pause for wind and sea's actions)* and the waves of the sea crashed. *(Pause for wind and sea's actions)* The sailors were afraid, *(Pause for sailors' actions)* and each one cried out for help. *(Pause for sailors' actions)*.

But the wind and sea raged on. *(Pause for wind and sea's actions)* So the sailors began throwing cargo from the ship into the sea to make the ship lighter. *(Pause for sailors' actions)*

Meanwhile, Jonah had gone far down inside the ship to lie down, *(Pause for Jonah's actions)* and he fell fast asleep. *(Pause for Jonah's actions)*

The sailors came to Jonah and said, "Why are you sleeping? Get up and pray to your god! Maybe then we won't die." *(Pause for sailors' actions)*

But the wind and sea continued their threat. *(Pause for wind and sea's actions)*

Jonah told the sailors that he had run away from God, *(Pause for Jonah's actions)* and the wind and sea became more angry. *(Pause for wind and sea's actions)* The sailors grew even more afraid. *(Pause for sailors' actions)*

Jonah said to the sailors, "Pick me up and throw me into the sea, and then it will calm down." Instead, the sailors tried to row the ship back to the land. *(Pause for sailors' actions)* But the wind and sea pushed the sailors back. *(Pause for wind and sea's and sailors' actions)*

The sailors cried to God to forgive them, *(Pause for sailors' actions)* and they threw Jonah into the raging sea. *(Pause for Jonah's and sailors' actions)* And the sea became calm. *(Pause for wind and sea's actions)*

God caused a big fish to swim toward Jonah, *(Pause for big fish's actions)* which swallowed him whole, in one giant, delicious gulp. *(Pause for big fish's and Jonah's actions)*

While Jonah was inside the fish, he prayed to God. *(Pause for Jonah's actions)* For three days he prayed to God. Then, on the third day, God spoke to the fish. The fish listened and spit Jonah onto the dry land. *(Pause for big fish's actions)*

God spoke to Jonah again and told him to go to the city of Nineveh and preach to the people there.

This time Jonah listened to God. *(Pause for Jonah's actions)* He never again wanted an up-close look inside a fish's mouth.

So Jonah entered the city and preached to the people of Nineveh. *(Pause for Jonah's actions)* Jonah shouted, "Repent and do good or after forty days, God will destroy Nineveh." *(Pause for Jonah's actions)*

The people of Nineveh were scared to death. *(Pause for people of Nineveh's actions)* They quit doing things they knew were wrong. *(Pause for people of Nineveh's actions)* They also stopped eating and put on rough, itchy clothes to show God their sadness for disobeying him. *(Pause for people of Nineveh's actions)*

As their stomachs gurgled and their skin itched, *(Pause for people of Nineveh's actions)* they turned toward God and cried out for God to save them. *(Pause for people of Nineveh's actions)* The people prayed and prayed to God. *(Pause for people of Nineveh's* actions) And they knelt down and worshiped him. *(Pause for people of Nineveh's actions)*

When God saw that the people had turned from their evil ways, God changed his mind and did not punish them.

But Jonah was very unhappy with God and jumped up and down angrily. *(Pause for Jonah's actions)* Jonah threw a tantrum and told God it wasn't fair that God had forgiven the people of Nineveh. *(Pause for Jonah's actions)* Jonah thought that the people of Nineveh should be punished.

And God said to Jonah, "Why shouldn't I show concern for the great city of Nineveh, which has more than 120,000 people?"

And so God forgave the people of Nineveh and did not destroy them.

BEFORE THE FINAL CURTAIN

Form four groups. Have each group read one chapter of Jonah and report back a summary of its chapter to everyone else. Next, have kids discuss these questions in their groups. Allow groups to share their responses with the rest of the people at the meeting.

1. God got Jonah's attention with a great fish. What does it take for God to get your attention? Why?

2. When was there a time you felt like Jonah? How did you respond?

3. When was a time you needed forgiveness like the people of Nineveh? What did you do about it?

4. Read Jonah 3:10 and Luke 23:32-34a. What do these passages tell us about forgiveness? Is there anything too great for God to forgive? Explain.

AFTER THE SHOW

Try these activities for further study.

1. Give each youth group member a paper plate, a tongue depressor, and colored markers. Have kids use their supplies to create a personal stop sign from God. Their signs might say "STOP and pray" or "STOP ignoring God." Encourage kids to use their signs as a reminder to follow God.

2. Have each youth group member write a definition of forgiveness and share it with the rest of the group. Then form a circle and have each person tell about a time when someone forgave him or her. Encourage kids to tell how they felt after the experience and how it affected their actions later. Finish with a prayer of thanks for God's never-ending forgiveness.

The First Noel

Theme:

THE BIRTH OF CHRIST

Scripture:

LUKE 2: 1–20

To the casual observer, Jesus' birth might have seemed insignificant. Just another Jewish baby—and this one born in a barn.

Who could've guessed that this "nobody" baby was really the richest person of all, the King of kings and Lord of lords—Jesus. And who knew that this "nobody" baby would someday make it possible for all of us to become "somebodies"?

Use this skit to help your kids become a part of the miraculous moment when Christ was born.

PROPS

For this skit you'll need

- a photocopy of the performance section of the skit.

SETTING THE STAGE

Before the meeting, read the entire skit at least once to become familiar with the story.

Select one volunteer to read the italicized portion of the skit while you read the plain text.

Form five groups (a group can be one person) and assign each group the following roles:

Group 1 ....Mary
Group 2 ....Joseph
Group 3 ....Shepherds
Group 4 ....Jesus
Group 5 ....Angel

Say: **I'm going to read a version of the Christmas story, based on the historical account in the book of Luke. Each time you hear your group's role mentioned, stand up and perform the actions of your assigned character.**

Teach kids the following cue words and actions to go with their roles:

Cue Words	Actions
MARY	Point to yourself and say, "Who? Me?"
JOSEPH	Shrug your shoulders and say, "What? Now?"
SHEPHERDS	Hold your nose and say, "Do I smell something?"
JESUS	Pantomime rocking a baby and then form a cross with your fingers and say, "Thank you, Lord."
ANGEL	Flap your arms like wings and say, "Hallelujah!"

Have groups practice their actions. Then read the skit and experience the reason we celebrate Christmas.

THE PERFORMANCE:
The First Noel

This is the story of the birth of *JESUS. JESUS'* mother, *MARY,* was engaged to *JOSEPH,* but before they got married, *MARY* was found to be pregnant through the Holy Spirit.

Sound unbelievable? Just think how Mary and Joseph felt. Anyway...

JOSEPH was a good man. *JOSEPH* didn't want to disgrace *MARY.* So *JOSEPH* was going to leave *MARY* quietly.

He must have been angry and disillusioned with her. Wouldn't you be? But let's get on with the story.

But an *ANGEL* appeared to *JOSEPH* in a dream and said, "*JOSEPH* don't be afraid to take *MARY* as your wife, because what is conceived in her is from the Holy Spirit. *MARY* will give birth to a son, and you are to give him the name *JESUS* because he will save his people from their sins."

Wow, the ANGEL came just in the nick of time. I wonder what happens next.

When *JOSEPH* woke up, he did what the *ANGEL* said and took *MARY* as his wife.

All right!

And in those days, Augustus Caesar declared all people must go to their hometown to be registered for a census. So *JOSEPH* and *MARY,* who was pregnant with *JESUS,* traveled to Bethlehem to be registered.

Great timing, huh? Can you imagine ... a very pregnant woman taking a long trip across a desert on foot? Ouch!

While *MARY* and *JOSEPH* were in Bethlehem, the time came for *JESUS* to be born. And *MARY* gave birth to a son, *JESUS*. *MARY* wrapped *JESUS* in cloths and placed *JESUS* in a manger because there was no room in the inn.

Yuck, a smelly animal trough, no sheets, no doctor, no hospital. She must have been scared. He must have been scared, too. No room at the inn. No room for the Son of God, the King of kings, the Lord of lords. Couldn't the innkeepers see the importance of that little baby? What a golden advertising opportunity those innkeepers missed! Imagine the billboard now—"Savior born in Hotel Bethlehem. Come and stay where the Christ child lay!"

Oh well, on with the story.

And there were *SHEPHERDS* watching their flocks in the fields nearby.

Disgusting people, those shepherds. They always smelled like sweaty sheep. Their workday was a killer, too. No eight-hour day for them. Day and night, feeding lambs, trying not to step on sheep dung, watching out for predators. Oops, time's a-wasting, and the story isn't finished yet!

An *ANGEL* appeared to the *SHEPHERDS,* and the *SHEPHERDS* were terrified.

Wouldn't you be? I'd be flat on the ground, nose first, in a dead faint!

But the *ANGEL* said to the *SHEPHERDS*, "Don't be afraid. I bring you good news of great joy. Today a Savior, *JESUS* has been born to you. You will find *JESUS* wrapped in cloths and lying in a manger."

I still can't believe the Savior of the world would be born in a manger, like some nameless, faceless nobody. A palace would be more appropriate, wouldn't it? Well, what happened next?

After the *ANGEL* left, the *SHEPHERDS* went to find the baby *JESUS* in the manger. When the *SHEPHERDS* found *MARY* and *JOSEPH* and *JESUS,* who was lying in the manger, the *SHEPHERDS* spread the word to all.

I wonder why God chose such lowly people to be the first witnesses of Jesus' birth?

And all who heard it were amazed at what the *SHEPHERDS* said about the baby named *JESUS,* who was born in a manger in Bethlehem.

You just can't figure out God. His very own Son—born to nobodies, in a nobody cow trough, and visited by the lowliest of nobodies. But then again, God thought all those people were definitely somebodies.

Hey, maybe, just maybe, I'm not a nobody to God either. Maybe I'm a somebody. Maybe I'm the reason Jesus came to earth in the first place.

And maybe you are, too. Merry Christmas.

BEFORE THE FINAL CURTAIN

Have groups read Luke 2:1–20 and discuss these questions.
1. How did you feel during the skit? Why? Who do you identify with most in the story? Why?
2. When do you feel like a nobody? What do you do during those times?
3. How do you think God feels about nobodies? How do you think God feels about you?
4. Jesus gave himself to you for Christmas. What will you give to him? Explain.

AFTER THE SHOW

Try these activities for further study.
1. Have kids brainstorm answers to this question: **What if Jesus had been born today instead of 2,000 years ago?** Encourage them to imagine where he might be born, what nationality he might be, and how the world would receive him.
2. Form a circle. Have kids take turns completing the following statement with one "feeling" word: *"God thinks I'm a somebody, and that makes me feel _____."*

Then have the group pray silently for "nobody" people who haven't yet heard they're somebodies to God. End the prayer with a group hug.

When You Pray...

Theme:
PRAYER

Scripture:
MATTHEW
6:9-13 AND
LUKE 11:5-13

*I*magine what life would be like if no one could pray. Knowing God had the power to work miracles and yet not being able to communicate with God would be frustrating, confusing, and unbearable.

Many junior highers face the prospect of prayer with similar feelings. They don't know how to talk to God and aren't sure God wants to hear what they have to say. As a result, many frustrated and confused junior highers simply give up on prayer.

Use this skit to help kids overcome negative feelings about prayer by learning how to communicate with their heavenly Father.

PROPS

For this skit you'll need

- a photocopy of the performance section of the skit.

SETTING THE STAGE

Before the meeting, read the entire skit at least once to become familiar with it. Also, select one volunteer to lead the pantomime actions and give him or her a photocopy of the performance section of the skit. Encourage your volunteer to read the skit beforehand and to practice the motions.

At the meeting have the group stand, facing you and your volunteer. Inform kids they will perform an echo-pantomime based on Matthew 6:9-13. Ask students to act out what you say by mimicking the volunteer's pantomime actions.

Tell kids this skit should be performed in complete silence. Then read the skit with feeling and at a steady pace. Be sure to allow enough time for students to mimic the volunteer and feel the emotion of the skit.

THE PERFORMANCE:
When You Pray...

The Script	The Actions
In this manner, therefore pray:	*Fold hands and bow head*
OUR FATHER	*Raise hands and look up in praise*
IN HEAVEN,	*Point up and swirl hands in the sky to suggest clouds*
HALLOWED BE YOUR NAME.	*Raise arms and bow from the waist*
YOUR KINGDOM COME.	*Make sweeping motion with one arm*
YOUR WILL BE DONE	*Point up, hit fists together, and outstretch hands with palms up*
ON EARTH	*Touch the ground with one finger*
AS IT IS IN HEAVEN.	*Point up and swirl hands in the sky to suggest clouds*
GIVE US THIS DAY	*Cup hands together to form a bowl*
OUR DAILY BREAD.	*Make eating motions*
AND FORGIVE US OUR DEBTS,	*Look up and wring hands*
AS WE FORGIVE OUR DEBTORS.	*Stretch out arms forward with palms up*
AND DO NOT LEAD US INTO TEMPTATION,	*Cover eyes with hands*
BUT DELIVER US FROM THE EVIL ONE.	*Hide face in hands and crouch in fear*
FOR YOURS	*Raise arms high in praise*
IS THE KINGDOM	*Sweep out with both arms, palms up*
AND THE POWER	*Swirl hands in circles as you raise arms high*

The Script	The Actions
AND THE GLORY FOREVER	*Applaud*
AMEN.	*Kneel on one knee, fold hands, and bow head*

(Matthew 6:9-13, New King James Version)

BEFORE THE FINAL CURTAIN

Have kids read Matthew 6:9-13 and Luke 11:5-13 and discuss these questions.
1. How did you feel during the skit? How do you feel when you pray?
2. How would you define "prayer"? Why should people pray? What kinds of things should be included in prayer?
3. What about prayer is hard for you? How can you overcome those obstacles?

AFTER THE SHOW

Try these activities for further study.
1. Form pairs and give each pair a photocopy of the "My Father" handout. Have kids create their own motions to the prayer on the handout and then perform them for the rest of the students.
2. Form four groups and give each group a map of the world. Have groups brainstorm needs that people might have in different parts of the world and then lead kids in praying for those needs.

My Father

Read the following paraphrase of the Lord's Prayer from Matthew 6:9-13 and write down one emotion you associate with each phrase. For example, you might write, "love" next to "My Father," or "awe" next to "You're worthy of all praise." Next, create new pantomime actions for the prayer that reflect those emotions.

Prayer	Emotion	Action
My Father		
In heaven,		
You're worthy of all praise.		
Bring your kingdom for me.		
Help me follow your will		
On earth		
Like angels follow your will in heaven.		
Provide for me today		
My daily needs.		
And please forgive the wrong things I've done,		
And help me forgive those who wrong me.		
Don't let temptation lead me away from you		
But protect me from Satan's schemes.		
For you have all authority,		
Power,		
And honor,		
Forever, Amen.		

Sow What?

Theme:

THE SOWER
AND THE SEED

Scripture:

MATTHEW
13:3-9 AND
13:18-23

*Y*ou *might not spot it at first. Spiritual growth in junior highers is often hidden behind the latest trends, feigned disinterest, or hot and cold spells of spiritual fervor.*

But chances are, if we look closely at our kids, we just might see signs indicating a growing relationship with God. We might spot growth that only God had noticed before.

Use this skit to encourage kids to bloom in their relationship with God.

PROPS

For this skit you'll need

- a photocopy of the performance section of the skit and
- five cue cards printed as follows:
  Cue Card 1......................."Applause"
  Cue Card 2......................."Amen"
  Cue Card 3......................."Too Bad"
  Cue Card 4......................."Get Outta Town"
  Cue Card 5......................."Switch"

SETTING THE STAGE

Before the meeting, read the entire skit at least once to become familiar with the story.

Select a volunteer to be in charge of flashing the appropriate cue cards during the skit. Give the volunteer a photocopy of the performance section of the skit so he or she can follow along with the story. Select two more volunteers to act as pantomime leaders for the skit. (If you have five or fewer junior highers, flash the cue cards yourself and have only one volunteer act as pantomime leader.)

Have the group stand, facing you and your volunteers. Say: **We're going to perform an echo-pantomime based on the story of the sower and the seed. As I read the skit, I'll pause for our pantomime leaders to make up and perform actions to illustrate the** story. Mimic their actions as best you can. And when a cue card is raised, do whatever it says. If you see the "switch" card, that means we'll need two new volunteers to lead the pantomime. Ready? Let's practice.

Have your volunteers do a few simple actions such as smiling or waving to allow kids to practice following their direction. Also, flash the cue cards and have kids practice responding to them.

Then read the skit enthusiastically. Be sure to pause where indicated for kids to perform their echo-pantomimes and allow time for kids to respond to the cue cards as they come up. If you'd like, use funny voices for the different characters and let kids know by your example it's okay to enjoy themselves during the performance.

THE PERFORMANCE:
Sow What?

Once there was a man who went into his field to sow seeds. *(Pause)* As he tossed seeds to and fro, *(Pause)* he sang to himself, *(Pause)*

"Sow, sow, sow my seed,

Evenly over my field;

Back and forth, and forth and back,

I pray for a good yield." *(Flash* Applause *cue card)*

And he spread his seeds all over. They floated through the air, *(Pause)* gyrating, *(Pause)* twisting, *(Pause)* turning. *(Pause)* Eventually all came to rest on the ground in all kinds of positions, looking as if they'd been playing a game of Twister. *(Pause)*

Some of the seeds fell along the road, where people walked and birds ate them. *(Pause)* The seeds tried frantically to dodge the feet and hungry birds *(Pause)* but couldn't avoid them all.

The seeds grumbled among themselves. "We hate it when that happens!" they said angrily. "So what if we wasn't exactly where we shoulda been? Does that mean we deserve to get stepped on and pecked at? *(Flash* Too Bad *cue card)* What should we have done? *(Flash* Get Outta Town *cue card)* Look, no matter how hard you try to do right, there's always some vulture out there ready to swoop down and sink his claws in ya! *(Flash* Too Bad *cue card)* Let's practice our fighter imitations; maybe that'll scare the birds away." *(Pause)*

But, in spite of their fierce fighter imitations, the last of the seeds by the road got carried away by the birds and could only play dead instead. *(Pause)* *(Flash* Switch *cue card)*

Some of the seeds fell *(Pause)* on rocky ground where there was little soil. The seeds soon sprouted *(Pause)* because the soil wasn't very deep. But when the sun came up, it burned the young plants. They cried and complained and had a little pity-party. *(Pause)* And since the roots hadn't grown deep enough, the plants soon dried up and blew away. *(Pause)* *(Flash* Switch *cue card)*

Some of the seeds fell *(Pause)* among the thorn bushes. The thorn bushes grew up and choked the seedlings with all the cares and concerns of this world. *(Pause)*

The thorns whispered things like, "You don't want to be caught dead with a hole in your underwear!" *(Flash* Amen *cue card)* and "Why aren't your clothes as nice as ours?" *(Flash* Too Bad *cue card)* and "I got more money than you got! Nyah, nyah, nyah, nyah!" *(Flash* Get Outta Town *cue card)*

And the seeds couldn't help themselves. They went shopping. *(Pause)* And skipped church. *(Flash* Too Bad *cue card)* And went shopping some more. *(Pause)* Before they knew it, they were buried under an avalanche of material things. *(Pause)* And soon they died for lack of air. *(Flash* Too Bad *cue card; flash* Switch *cue card)*

But some of the seeds fell *(Pause)* in good soil, and the plants sprouted! *(Pause)* *(Flash* Applause *cue card; flash* Amen *cue card)*

Some friends were sarcastic about it. They twiddled their fingers and said, "Whoop-de-do," *(Pause)* *(Flash* Too Bad *cue card)* and put their hands over their hearts and said, "Isn't that special!" *(Pause)* *(Flash* Get Outta Town *cue card)*

But the Sower was excited about these seeds. He danced and twirled for joy. *(Pause)* *(Flash* Applause *cue card)* He watered and cared for the seeds, *(Pause)* guarded them from harm, *(Pause)* and helped them produce 30, 60, and 100 times more food than they thought possible. *(Flash* Applause *cue card)*

Now, the question remains: Are you the kind of person the Sower would get excited about?

BEFORE THE FINAL CURTAIN

Have kids read Matthew 13:3-9 and 13:18-23 and discuss these questions.

1. Which character in the skit do you relate to most? Why?
2. Have you ever felt like the seeds surrounded by thorns? Explain.
3. What are specific things we can do to help one another grow like seeds planted in good soil?

AFTER THE SHOW

Try these activities for further study.

1. Have your youth group plant a garden on the church property. Let kids choose what types of plants or flowers to include in the garden. Then have groups of students commit to caring for the garden on weekly intervals.

After your garden has bloomed (or died!) have kids discuss what it took for their garden to remain healthy and what happened to harm it. Then discuss what it takes for Christians to remain healthy and how to protect against the harmful aspects of life.

2. Have kids interview older members in your church. Have them ask the following questions:
   - **If you had to describe your faith journey as a plant, what plant would you choose and why?**
   - **What has been the toughest part of living the Christian faith for you?**
   - **What has been the most rewarding aspect of living the Christian life for you?**

Have kids share their interview results with the entire youth group and then discuss how they would answer those same questions.

Golf Cart Missionaries

Theme:

PAUL AND
SILAS IN THE
PHILIPPIAN
PRISON

Scripture:

ACTS 16:6-40

Warning: *Being a Christian junior higher can be hazardous to your health. Junior highers face daily struggles as they try to live a Christian life. Friends ridicule their faith. Television and movies encourage non-Christian behavior. And enemies brand them as hypocrites for the slightest failure.*

Yet, Jesus never said, "Follow me until it gets tough" or "Follow me as long as it's convenient." He simply said, "Follow me."

Use this skit to help students explore the risks and rewards of serving God.

PROPS

No props are needed for this skit.

SETTING THE STAGE

Before the meeting, read the entire skit at least once to become familiar with the story.

At the meeting, select two volunteers to play the roles of Pat and Terry. These can be either guys or girls. Tell your volunteers to act out everything you say about them during the skit.

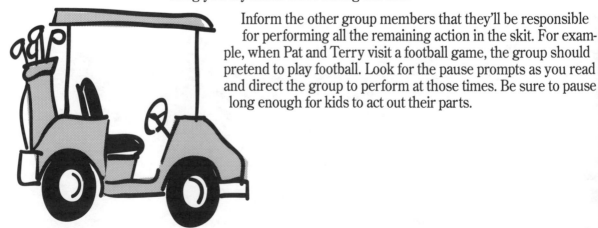

Inform the other group members that they'll be responsible for performing all the remaining action in the skit. For example, when Pat and Terry visit a football game, the group should pretend to play football. Look for the pause prompts as you read and direct the group to perform at those times. Be sure to pause long enough for kids to act out their parts.

THE PERFORMANCE:
Golf Cart Missionaries

Once there were two Christians, Pat and Terry, who wanted others to know about Jesus and his love. They decided to go to as many sporting events as they could and tell the people about Jesus.

They visited football games. *(Pause and direct group to perform)* They attended basketball games. *(Pause and direct group to perform)* Once or twice, they made it to a wrestling match. *(Pause and direct group to perform)* They even took in some gymnastics. *(Pause and direct group to perform)*

By going to all these events, Pat and Terry soon were pretty well-known. Many people looked forward to seeing them because they wanted to know more about Jesus. No matter what sporting event they went to, Pat and Terry would always draw a crowd around them. *(Pause and direct group to perform)* Pat and Terry took the opportunity to answer questions or tell what they knew about God's love to everyone they met. They even signed a few autographs. *(Pause, direct Pat, Terry, and group to perform)*

Other people weren't so thrilled about Pat and Terry's showing up at their sporting events. They grumbled angrily and frowned at Pat and Terry. *(Pause and direct group to perform)*

One day, Pat and Terry showed up at a golf tournament. *(Pause and direct group to perform)* You know how everyone always whispers at golf tournaments, even when they're on television? *(Pause and direct group to perform)* Well, just as the biggest hotshot golfer was about to make his winning stroke, the crowd yelled, "Hey! There are those two Christians, Pat and Terry!" *(Pause and direct group to perform)*

Of course, this made the hotshot golfer miss the ball entirely and lose millions of dollars in prize money. In his anger, the hotshot golfer called security and had Pat and Terry arrested for disrupting the golf match. *(Pause, direct Pat, Terry, and group to perform)*

Since no jail was available, the security officers locked Pat and Terry in the garage where all the golf carts were parked. *(Pause, direct Pat, Terry, and group to perform)* The only other people in the garage were golf cart mechanics, getting ready to go home. Unfortunately, they were now locked in the garage for the night with Pat and Terry. The golf cart mechanics weren't too happy about that. *(Pause and direct group to perform)*

Pat and Terry decided to make the best of the situation. They shook hands with everyone and introduced themselves. *(Pause, direct Pat and Terry to perform)* Pat and Terry thought about leading a Bible study, but the mechanics shook their heads; *(Pause and direct group to perform)* they weren't interested. The mechanics settled down on the floor and tried to get comfortable. *(Pause and direct group to perform)*

But Pat and Terry weren't tired. They were glad God had put them in this greasy garage. They began to sing "Jesus Loves Me" at the top of their lungs. *(Pause and direct Pat and Terry to perform)* The mechanics all covered their ears and complained, *(Pause and direct group to perform)* but our heroes kept it up, singing even louder! *(Pause, direct Pat and Terry to perform)*

After a few minutes, some of the mechanics started listening to the words of the song. *(Pause and direct group to perform)* They wondered how anyone could sing while locked up in a cold cement garage with axle grease all over the floor. Pretty soon, everyone was sitting up and listening to Pat and Terry. *(Pause and direct group to perform)*

All of a sudden, an earthquake hit! Everyone was swaying *(Pause, direct Pat, Terry, and group to perform)* and shaking *(Pause, direct Pat, Terry, and group to perform)* and shaking *(Pause, direct Pat, Terry, and group to perform)* and swaying. *(Pause, direct Pat, Terry, and group to perform)* The walls of the garage fell down, and everyone huddled together *(Pause, direct Pat, Terry, and group to perform)* to keep from being hit by bricks. When the dust finally settled, everyone could see that the garage had been entirely destroyed. Miraculously, no one had been hurt!

The hotshot golfer showed up just then. He felt awful for having locked everyone up and was worried someone might have been hurt. He was also worried he'd made God angry by picking on Pat and Terry. When the hotshot golfer saw Pat and Terry, he fell on his knees and asked them to tell him about Jesus.

Everyone gathered around as Pat and Terry shared the message of God's love. *(Pause, direct Pat, Terry, and group to perform)* The mechanics—and even the hotshot golfer—decided to become followers of Christ. *(Pause and direct group to perform)* They started a new church right there among the golf carts and called it God's Greasy Garage.

Everyone was so happy they all sang "Jesus Loves Me" at the top of their lungs. *(Pause, direct Pat, Terry, and group to perform)* Thankfully, there wasn't an earthquake that time.

BEFORE THE FINAL CURTAIN

Have kids read Acts 16:6-40 and discuss these questions.

1. How would you have responded in Pat and Terry's or Paul and Silas' situation? How would you have responded if there hadn't been an earthquake after all?
2. What do you do when people ask you about your faith? What do you do when they ridicule your faith?
3. What are the risks of sharing your faith with someone who isn't a Christian? How much risk are you willing to take?
4. What are the rewards of sharing your faith?

AFTER THE SHOW

Try these activities for further study.

1. Have kids follow the example of Paul and Silas by visiting a local prison and conducting a church service for the inmates. Have your group sing some of its favorite Christian songs. Then have two or three kids share a few minutes on the theme "What Jesus means to me."
2. Hold a Christian trial. Have kids anonymously write down five things that could be used as evidence in court to prove they're Christians. Then collect all the lists and read them to the group. Have the group vote on whether or not they would "convict" a person of being a Christian based on that person's list.

Afterward, discuss what evidence non-Christians need in order to see Jesus living in us.

SECTION II.

Skits on Hot Topics

Can't Hear You in Wagamazoo!

Theme:
LISTENING

Scripture:
1 KINGS 19:11-18 AND PSALMS 46:10-11

Did you hear that?

Shhh. Listen.

What do you hear? A radio blaring? Traffic noisily making its way down the street? People yelling? A television blaring? Fans blowing?

When was the last time you stopped to listen—and heard the voice of God? When was the last time your group members did?

Use this skit to help your kids become aware of the still, small voice of God that speaks in the quiet of the heart.

PROPS

No props are needed for this skit.

SETTING THE STAGE

Before the meeting, read the entire skit at least once to become familiar with the story.

Have kids number off from one to six and form groups based on their numbers. Assign groups the following roles:

Ones	Motormouths
Twos	Talkers
Threes	Tooters
Fours	Bangers
Fives	Clangers
Sixes	Snoozers

Have kids work together to come up with a unique sound effect for their group's character. Encourage students to be creative and unusual, without being crude. Tell them to be sure everyone in their group is involved in the sound effects they create.

Then have kids mingle and form a circle. Encourage kids to stand next to people from other groups.

Say: **We're going to perform the skit** *Can't Hear You in Wagamazoo.* **You all know your parts, so each time you hear me say your character's name, perform your sound effect as loudly as possible. In addition, each time I pause and raise my hand, that'll be your cue to make a sound effect for the word I just read. I'll lower my hand when it's time to stop the sound effect. Ready? Let's practice.**

Have kids practice their sound effects at least once before you begin. For the practice, say the name of each group's role, raise your hand, and have the appropriate group members perform their sounds. After all groups have had a chance to practice, read the skit. Don't forget to pause for sound effects each time you see an italicized word.

THE PERFORMANCE:
Can't Hear You in Wagamazoo!

As the sun peeked through the early morning sky in the town of Wagamazoo, the *MOTORMOUTHS* rose from their night's sleep. Alarm clocks *buzzed* furiously, feet *pounded* the floor, water *gurgled* through the pipes, and parents *screamed* for their children to hurry up.

CLANGERS, TALKERS, TOOTERS, and *BANGERS* also started their day amidst the noise. Grandfather clocks *gonged,* car horns *honked,* and babies *cried* for their food. All over town the hustle and bustle of morning could be heard.

The wind *whistled* through the trees, rain *banged* endlessly on the tin roofs, and impatient *TALKERS* yelled over the phone at the *BANGERS. TOOTERS screeched* their brakes to a grinding halt as they picked up the *CLANGERS* for work. It was a day just like any other in Wagamazoo.

Except—the *BUZZERS* were still asleep.

Usually the *whistle* of the train woke them. Sometimes the cars *honking* or brakes *screeching* was enough to jar them from their sleep. If these things couldn't rouse them, the s*naps, shrieks, clangs,* and *thumps* from Factory Wagamazoo always did the job.

Until today.

In spite of all this noise, the *BUZZERS* were still *snoring* in bed. No parents *yelled,* no radios *blared,* no televisions *droned,* and no toilets *flushed.*

At Factory Wagamazoo, chaos broke loose. *MOTORMOUTHS screamed* to *TOOTERS. TALKERS cried* to *BANGERS. CLANGERS shouted* at everyone, "Where are the *BUZZERS?* We can't work without them!"

The pipes at Factory Wagamazoo *hissed,* the great gears *squeaked,* and the pistons *hammered* and *clanked. TOOTERS* didn't listen to *MOTORMOUTHS. BANGERS* never heard the *TALKERS.* And *CLANGERS* were simply ignored. Everyone ran around, *shouting* and *whistling* and generally getting nothing done.

What had happened? What hideous crime had befallen the *BUZZERS* that caused them to miss work?

It was no devious plot. The *BUZZERS* weren't at work because of the bitter cold. The previous night, while pans *clanked* in the sink, parents *yelled* about homework, nightly news *droned* on the televisions, and airplanes *thundered* overhead, the *BUZZERS* had put on their earmuffs to keep their ears warm. And they had forgotten to take them off before bedtime. They slumbered blissfully through the morning *noise.*

At six minutes after nine, the littlest *BUZZER* began to stir. He thought he was dreaming. He had never heard *silence* before.

"What do you do when it's quiet? And why is it so quiet?" he wondered. It seemed so peaceful. No train *whistling,* no horns *honking,* no *MOTORMOUTHS* yelling, no alarm clocks *ringing,* no boom boxes *booming,* no *snapping, clanging* or *thumping* from the factory. Just blessed, peaceful *silence.*

Surprised, he awoke his parents. They, too, were amazed by the *silence.* One by one the *BUZZERS* woke, and one by one they sat in wonder at the beauty of the *silence.* And in the quiet, they began to hear the *whisper* of God sharing his message of love.

Then the first earmuffs came off.

Others soon took off their earmuffs, too. Before long, the whisper was forgotten and the silence left behind. Telephones *rang,* people *screamed,* televisions *blared,* vacuum cleaners *hummed,* babies *cried,* and horns *beeped,* as the *BUZZERS* hurried to get to work.

The *BUZZERS screamed* at one another all the way to the factory. And when they arrived there was so much *banging* and *clanking* that it took hours for the *MOTORMOUTHS, TALKERS, TOOTERS, BANGERS,* and *CLANGERS* to even realize the *BUZZERS* had reported to work.

After that morning, all went on as usual in Wagamazoo. *Noise* ruled. Creation's echo and the voice of God were lost in the *roar* of daily living.

Except now, once a year, the *BUZZERS* remember that time of *silence* and celebrate by wearing earmuffs all day long.

Funny thing—the *BUZZERS* say they hear more on that day than they do throughout the rest of the year.

Once a year, they listen in Wagamazoo. How often do you?

BEFORE THE FINAL CURTAIN

Have kids read 1 Kings 19:11-18 and Psalms 46:10-11 and discuss these questions.

1. How did you feel during the skit? Explain. How is Wagamazoo similar to or different from your experience?

2. What does it take to really communicate with God? What "noises" drown out God's voice in your life?

3. Why is it important to be still and listen to God?

4. What would your life be like if God never listened to you? How does knowing that God does listen affect the way you live?

AFTER THE SHOW

Try these activities for further study.

1. Have kids listen to the sounds of silence. Give each student a sheet of paper and a pencil. Instruct the group to be absolutely silent for two minutes. When two minutes are up, tell kids to write everything they heard during the two minutes, such as a friend breathing or air conditioner vents blowing.

Next have kids brainstorm ways they can hear God speaking to them in the silence, such as through the Bible or through nature.

2. Form groups of no more than five and have each group write down 10 commandments of good listening. Tell groups to include commandments to encourage good listening traits and to discourage poor listening habits.

Have groups compare ideas and discuss why they wrote what they did. Challenge kids to live out their commandments in their relationships with God, family, and friends.

The Driving Zone

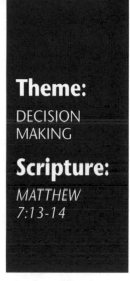

Theme:
DECISION MAKING

Scripture:
MATTHEW 7:13-14

The choices a junior higher makes today will undoubtedly influence the direction his or her life will take tomorrow.

Unfortunately, many junior highers race down the road of life oblivious to God's warning signs in scripture. The results are lives impaired by drugs and alcohol, materialistic values, and increasingly selfish lifestyles.

Use this skit to help kids recognize God's warning signs so they can make wise decisions as they travel the road of life.

PROPS

For this skit you'll need

- 12 sheets of newsprint and
- three markers.

SETTING THE STAGE

Before the meeting, read the entire skit at least once to become familiar with the story.

Form three groups. Give each group four sheets of newsprint and a marker. Tell groups to create four highway warning signs. Encourage kids to be creative in their sign making. For example, they might make a sign that reads, "Danger: Godzilla Crossing" or " Wrong Way—Unless You Like Tar Pits." When groups are finished, mix up the signs and place them face down in a pile next to you.

Say (dramatically, as in an introduction to the *Twilight Zone*): **Group 1, you are the Nancy Toxicated family. Group 2, you are the Nathan Style family. Group 3, you are the Ben Bickering family. And you're all about to enter... the Driving Zone. Each of you is traveling with your family. Your destination: the Pearly Gates. Listen carefully and act out the events as they happen to your family. I'll pause when it's time to perform. Now, on to... the Driving Zone!**

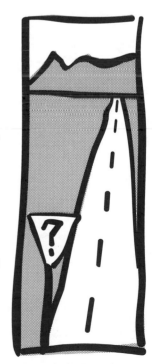

As you read the performance section, be sure to pause where indicated to allow groups to act out their parts. Also, when you see a prompt for a road sign in the skit, show kids one from your pile of newsprint signs. Don't worry if the signs don't seem to make sense—they'll just add to the fun of the show!

THE PERFORMANCE:
The Driving Zone

It's early in the day when the Toxicated family awakens from their slumber. Stretching and yawning, *(Pause)* they slowly gather their bags, lug them to their '79 Pinto wagon, *(Pause)* and speed down the highway. *(Pause)*

On a whim, the Toxicateds choose what looks to be a well-paved road that will lead them to the Pearly Gates. *(Pause)* Soon, they come to a road sign. *(Read* Road Sign #1)

What will they do? We'll have to find out later because...

It's just after lunch, and the Styles model their vacation outfits one more time, glamorously twirling and strutting their stuff. *(Pause)* Cheering one another on, *(Pause)* they pretend to walk a model's fashion runway. *(Pause)* Only the finest clothes should be taken on their trip to the Pearly Gates.

Then the Styles drag their heavy luggage to the Ferrari minivan and depart. *(Pause)* They decide on the easiest path to the Pearly Gates—the one most frequently traveled. *(Pause)* On the wide, straight road the Styles stop to look at a road sign. *(Read* Road Sign #2) They laugh at the warning *(Pause)* and speed on their way, right past the Bickering family's house...

Late in the day, the Bickerings are finally ready to leave. Pushing and shoving one another, *(Pause)* they fight over the back seat of their refurbished school bus. The biggest one wins, *(Pause)* and the rest grumble as they find other seats. *(Pause)* They pull onto the road, and the young Bickerings jump up and down inside the bus to see if they can tip it over. *(Pause)* Just then the older Bickerings spot a road through the cliffs and cheer. *(Pause)* Everyone sees a warning sign, *(Read* Road Sign #3) but they continue down the road anyway.

Meanwhile, the Toxicated family continues their journey. It's been hours since they began the trip, and family members are thirsty. *(Pause)*

"Not to worry," says the oldest Toxicated, "I've brought something that'll make you forget what water tastes like!"

From under the seat the Toxicated elder pulls out a case of Smeer, *(Pause)* the better tasting but less filling alcoholic drink of champions. As bottles are passed to each family member, *(Pause)* the driver slows to read a warning sign on the road. *(Read* Road Sign #4) The Toxicateds just giggle and ask for more drinks. *(Pause)*

At the same time, the Styles open their eyes wide in amazement as they travel. *(Pause)* The road is beautiful. They blink at the glittering diamonds scattered in the cement. *(Pause)* They wave to all the other cars and buses they pass. *(Pause)* Before long, they slow down and read another road sign. *(Read* Road Sign #5)

They shake their heads, *(Pause)* laugh, *(Pause)* and continue down their diamond-studded road. They open the windows, sniff loudly, *(Pause)* and smile with pleasure at the perfumed aroma— until they see the next road sign. *(Read* Road Sign #6) Still, they drive on, wondering what the Bickerings are doing…

As the Bickerings drive through the mountains, they begin to argue and yell, *(Pause)* until another warning sign comes into view. The driver slams on the breaks, and everyone goes flying. *(Pause)* They read the worn-out sign. *(Read* Road Sign #7)

Just 100 feet down the road, they spot another sign and read it. *(Read* Road Sign #8) They're angry and in a hurry, so they simply ignore it. To the left and to the right, they navigate the hairpin turns of the cliffs. *(Pause)* Only a few more miles…

The Toxicated family drives slowly since their eyesight has become blurry. At the bottom of a hill, they encounter another road sign. *(Read* Road Sign #9) But they can't make out what it says, so they giggle *(Pause)* and drive on. As they drive, they continually point at objects outside the car and giggle hysterically. *(Pause)* Their drunken haze makes everything look funny.

Without warning, the road veers to the right. Several members of the Toxicated family get sick in the back seat as the Pinto barely makes the turn. *(Pause)* Someone sees another road sign *(Read* Road Sign #10), but they're all feeling sick now, and no one wants to read while the car is moving. *(Pause)*

Soon they're within view of the Pearly Gates. They drink one last toast to celebrate, but no one sees the final curve. *(Pause)* The Toxicated family is killed instantly as the car smashes into the mountainside, ending their trip in tragedy.

The shimmering of the jewels in the road has made the Style family sleepy. *(Pause)* Jerking their heads up, *(Pause)* they pry open their eyes *(Pause)* and try to stay awake. A sign appears in the distance *(Read* Road Sign #11), but they're too sleepy to read it.

Someone spots a party at a rest stop ahead, and everyone suddenly awakens. They stop, rummage through their suitcases, *(Pause)* put on their finest outfits, *(Pause)* and join the party. They strut their stuff, *(Pause)* wiggle their hips, *(Pause)* pucker their lips, *(Pause)* and fit right in. The Styles become so wrapped up in their party that they completely forget that the Pearly Gates await them. Many years later their Ferrari is found, rusted and abandoned, among the smoking remains of what once was a party.

The Bickering family nears their journey's end. The gates are within view when they happen upon one more road sign. *(Read* Road Sign #12) Everyone is grumpy *(Pause)* and wants to arrive as quickly as possible. But as the driver turns to slap a passenger in the back seat, *(Pause)* he doesn't notice the upcoming curve. The Bickerings scream *(Pause)* as they travel through the air and over the cliff. The Bickering family's trip is abruptly halted at the bottom of the cliff.

Three families, similar fates. All because they couldn't read the signs in ... the Driving Zone.

BEFORE THE FINAL CURTAIN

Have kids read Matthew 7:13-14 and discuss these questions.
1. How did you feel during your "road trip" to the Pearly Gates? What were the poor decisions the families made in this skit? What are some warning signs God gives to help us make wise decisions in life?
2. Why do you think Jesus says the road to heaven and true life is narrow? How do you think a person gets on this road to heaven?
3. What part does decision making play in our journey toward heaven? How can we make wise decisions? What are the rewards of making wise decisions?

AFTER THE SHOW

Try these activities for further study.
1. Take your group go-cart racing. Observe the habits and driving styles of your students. Afterward, ask students what their lives would be like if they reflected their driving styles. Encourage kids to consider how they'd drive if they had a special friend riding with them. Then

have them discuss how they should "drive" their lives, knowing that Jesus is always with them.

2. Give each student a 3×5 card and a pencil. Have kids each make a mock driver's license, complete with a hand-drawn picture and vital statistics. On the back of their drivers' licenses have kids write out Matthew 7:13-14. Tell kids to take their licenses home as a reminder to look for Jesus' warning signs when faced with a decision.

How Do You Spell Relief?

Theme:
PEER PRESSURE

Scripture:
ROMANS 12:2

Wouldn't it be great if negative peer pressure could be cured with a visit to a doctor's office?

Unfortunately, a doctor can't cure a junior higher's struggle with negative peer pressure. But Jesus can. Use this skit to show kids how Jesus can help them deal positively with the problem of negative peer pressure.

PROPS

No props are needed for this skit.

SETTING THE STAGE

Before the meeting, read the entire skit at least once to become familiar with the story.

Select one volunteer to lead the pantomime actions during the first portion of the skit. At the places indicated, have the pantomime leader switch places with someone else in the group. If you have fewer than six group members, have some kids repeat as pantomime leaders.

Have the group stand, facing you and your volunteer. Say: **We're going to perform an echo-pantomime titled** *How Do You Spell Relief?* **As I read the skit, I'll pause for our pantomime leader to make up and perform actions to illustrate the story. Try to mimic his or her actions as best you can. We'll switch pantomime leaders every time I clap my hands. Ready? Let's get started!**

Read the skit with plenty of enthusiasm. Be sure to pause where indicated for kids to perform their echo-pantomimes.

THE PERFORMANCE:
How Do You Spell Relief?

One day a young man crawled into the doctor's office complaining of severe pains. *(Pause)* He had a blank look in his eyes and a slack jaw. *(Pause)* It was quite evident that he was suffering from negative peer pressure.

The man had an annoying habit of mimicking others around him. For instance, when he spied the older gentleman with the twitching eyebrows, he decided that was the thing to do. *(Pause)* When he noticed the woman next to him constantly glancing at her watch, he thought that made her look pretty important. So he started doing the same thing, because he wanted to look important, too. *(Pause)* It didn't seem to matter to the man with negative peer pressure that he wasn't wearing a watch. This was definitely a case of acute negative peer pressure! *(Clap hands to signal kids to switch pantomime leaders)*

A little boy played with toy cars on the floor of the doctor's office. The attention the little boy received from others in the room was more than the man could handle. Suddenly he dropped to the floor on all fours *(Pause)* and started racing a toy firetruck back and forth across the carpet, *(Pause)* making the same siren noises the little boy was making. *(Pause)*

When he saw the disapproval of the others in the waiting room, the man jumped up and sat back in his chair, thoroughly embarrassed. *(Pause)* His now deadpan face resumed its nervous twitching with even greater intensity. *(Pause)* *(Clap hands to signal kids to switch pantomime leaders)*

Finally, the man was called into the examining room, much to the relief of the other patients in the waiting room. The man proceeded to describe his unbearable negative peer pressure to the doctor. *(Pause)*

"Doctor, I don't know what comes over me," he said. "I feel this incredible negative peer pressure whenever I'm in a group. If someone in the group starts licking his or her nose, I start licking mine, too. *(Pause)*

"If my friends do Elvis imitations, I do them, too. *(Pause)* If someone offers me a cigarette, I light up. *(Pause)* If they pour me a drink, I gulp it down and ask for another! *(Pause)* And, Doc, I don't smoke or drink!" the man said in a tone of despair.

"It's terrible when I go out in public," he continued. "When I see couples holding hands, I hold hands with myself. *(Pause)* If I see a monkey at a zoo, I can't keep myself from scratching my back and saying 'Hoo-hoo-haa-haa.' *(Pause)* If I watch a sporting event, I run around and flex my muscles. *(Pause)* Oh, Doc, what will I do?" *(Clap hands to signal kids to switch pantomime leaders)*

The doctor propped his chin in his hand to think. As if by reflex, the man with negative peer pressure did the same thing. *(Pause)* Then the doctor stroked his face thoughtfully, and the furrows in his brow deepened. The man, without thinking, started stroking his own face and wrinkling his brow. *(Pause)*

Finally the doctor said, "It's my professional opinion that you have the severest form of negative peer pressure I've ever seen—mimicitus dangerosis. To be quite blunt about it, you've lost your mind. *(Pause)* You're out of control. *(Pause)* Lie down now. *(Pause)* I must operate."

The man lay down and then stood back up. *(Pause)* "But I'm afraid of surgery," he said. *(Pause)*

"Lie down," *(Pause)* said the doctor. "You need a new heart. One that isn't intimidated by the crowd. One that communicates love to yourself and others. You can't get that unless I operate."

The man stood up again. *(Pause)* "Wait a minute!" he said. "Isn't there some other way?" He was starting to get frantic. *(Pause)* *(Clap hands to signal kids to switch pantomime leaders)*

"All right," said the doctor. "Do this. First, run in place for five seconds. *(Pause)* Then touch your toes twice. *(Pause)* Next, spin around in a circle three times. (Pause) Finally, do five jumping jacks. *(Pause)* Now, are you cured?"

"No, just sweaty," replied the man. "Oh, woe is me!" he said and started crying like a baby. *(Pause)*

The doctor sighed, "Just as I thought. You've become like a cheap beef stew—mostly vegetable and very little meat. People smell you coming and say, 'Mm-Mm bad.' Unless you get a new heart, you're destined to follow the crowd for the rest of your life."

When the nurse came in with a surgical knife, the man shook in his shoes. *(Pause)*

"Just a moment, Doctor," she said. "You don't have to cut his heart out to cure him from negative peer pressure. Jesus can put in a new heart without surgery."

The man jumped up and down happily. *(Pause)* "I like it! I like it!" he shouted. *(Pause)* *(Clap hands to signal kids to switch pantomime leaders)*

"But how will that help him overcome negative peer pressure?" asked the doctor. "Will it make him strong like a lion?" *(Pause)*

"It will help him learn that Jesus loves him no matter what others think," said the nurse. "And it will help him stand firm in the face of opposition, because he'll know that Jesus will stand with him." *(Pause)*

"Sounds perfect," said the man as he mimicked the nurse's smile. *(Pause)* "How do I do it?"

"It's simple, really," said the nurse. "Just ask."

The man slapped his forehead. *(Pause)* "Now why didn't I think of that?" he said.

Then he bowed his head *(Pause)* and prayed, "Jesus, I've messed up by following the crowd instead of you. Please forgive me and help me to focus my sights on you. Amen." *(Pause)*

BEFORE THE FINAL CURTAIN

Have kids read Romans 12:2 and discuss these questions.
1. How is the man in this skit like someone who changes or conforms to people in the world? How are you like the man in the skit?
2. What advice would you give to someone struggling with negative peer pressure? How can peer pressure be a positive thing?
3. Why is it important to follow Jesus instead of the crowd? Why are we tempted to follow the crowd? How can we help each other to follow Jesus?

AFTER THE SHOW

Try these activties for further study.
1. Take your youth group people-watching. Go to a nearby mall or shopping center and have your kids form pairs. Give each pair a pencil and a sheet of paper and instruct them to observe people for the next half-hour. Tell them to record examples they see of people's conforming to peer pressure. For example, if they see a group of kids dressed the same way or a group of people doing the same thing, they should write it down.

Afterward, have kids discuss the seen and unseen influences of peer pressure.

2. Form groups of no more than three. Have each group complete the

following sentences: **"Three ways we can be positive influences on our friends are . . . "** and **"Three ways we can influence others to build a relationship with Jesus are . . . "**

Have groups pick a spokesperson to share their responses with the rest of the students.

Just a Rose

Theme:
SEXUALITY

Scripture:
ROMANS
6:12-14; 2
CORINTHIANS
5:17; AND
EPHESIANS 5:1-3

Kids in your group may be sexually active.

It's hard to believe, but statistics show that by the time Christian teenagers reach 18, 43 percent will have had premarital sexual intercourse. The threat of pregnancy, AIDS, and other sexually transmitted diseases is enough to make some junior highers put off having sex. But there is a bigger issue involved—the worth of one's own sexuality.

Losing virginity is permanent. God offers forgiveness, but he will not "undo" what has been done. When a person becomes sexually involved, he or she gives away something that can never be retrieved. Use this skit to help students understand the value of their gift of sexuality.

PROPS

For this skit you'll need

- one red rose (without thorns),
- one pink rose (without thorns), and
- two gift boxes.

SETTING THE STAGE

Before the meeting, read the entire skit at least once to become familiar with the story. Make sure the content is appropriate for your group's maturity level. Be aware of kids who may have strong reactions to the skit due to past sexual abuse or promiscuity and be prepared to counsel with them afterward. For the skit you'll also need to wrap a rose in each of the gift boxes.

Form two groups—one group of guys and one group of girls. Select one guy volunteer to play the part of "Steve" and one girl volunteer to play "Denise." Give Steve the box with the red rose and Denise the box with the pink rose.

Have each group form a circle, with Steve standing in the middle of the guys' circle and Denise standing in the middle of the girls' circle.

Say: **We're going to perform the skit** *Just a Rose.* **As I read the skit, I'll pause to allow you to act out the story. The guys' group should act out anything referring to them, and the girls' group should do the same. Steve and Denise will perform actions that relate to them as well. Ready? Let's begin.**

THE PERFORMANCE:
Just a Rose

Once upon a time, God wanted to give something special to his children, Steve and Denise. So he gave each of them a gift box with a surprise inside.

Steve was pretty excited. He tried to peek through the wrapping *(Pause for Steve's actions)* but couldn't tell what was inside. He shook the package to see if he could figure out what was inside. *(Pause for Steve's actions)* Finally he ripped the package open, *(Pause for Steve's actions)* and inside was a red rose.

Denise was also very curious about her present. *(Pause for Denise's actions)* She balanced it on her head to see if it was heavy. *(Pause for Denise's actions)* It wasn't. She tossed it in the air to see if it would break. *(Pause for Denise's actions)* It didn't. Finally, she too ripped open her package, *(Pause for Denise's actions)* and inside was a pink rose.

God spoke to his children. "For years, guys and girls have been very confused about each other. *(Pause for guys' and girls' actions)* They needed a special gift, a present from me to show how much I value them. So, I gave them their sexuality.

"Your roses, Steve and Denise, are symbols of that sexuality. Treasure them and care for them so that when you marry you'll have a special gift to give your husband or wife for the rest of your life."

So Steve and Denise hid their roses in safe places. *(Pause for Steve's and Denise's actions)*

Time passed. Denise met quite a few guys. *(Pause for guys' and Denise's actions)* Sometimes she'd get other girls to go out on group dates with her and other guys. *(Pause for guys', girls', and Denise's actions)* They'd usually go out to eat *(Pause for guys', girls', and Denise's actions)* and then to a movie *(Pause for guys', girls', and Denise's actions)* or dancing. *(Pause for guys', girls', and Denise's actions)* All in all, Denise and the girls had a pretty good time.

Steve spent a lot of time with girls. Sometimes he'd get a group of guys together, and they'd serenade the girls while kneeling on one knee. *(Pause for guys', girls,' and Steve's actions)* Other times, the guys would try to show off for the girls by playing basketball *(Pause for guys' and Steve's actions)* or football *(Pause for guys' and Steve's actions)* or a musical instrument. *(Pause for guys' and Steve's actions)* The girls always "oohed" and "aahed" appreciatively. *(Pause for girls' actions)*

The girls especially liked it when Steve and the guys would invite them to the mall. *(Pause for guys', girls', and Steve's actions)* They'd all go window shopping, *(Pause for guys', girls', and Steve's actions)* play video games, *(Pause for guys', girls', and Steve's actions)* and eat onion rings in the food court. *(Pause for guys', girls', and Steve's actions)*. All in all, it was a pretty fun experience.

Then one day Steve picked out a special girl from among the other girls. *(Pause for Steve's and girl's actions)* They started going out and, pretty soon, were seeing each other often. *(Pause for Steve and girl's actions)* They dated for several months, and all the guys, girls, and Denise whispered to one another that Steve and this girl would get married. *(Pause for everyone's actions)*

Once, while they were out on a date, this girl asked if Steve would give her his rose. Steve was tempted, but he remembered what God had said about saving it for his wife, *(Pause for Steve's actions)* so he refused. The girl cried and threw a fit, but still Steve refused. That night, Steve and the girl broke up. *(Pause for Steve's and girl's actions)*

The next day, all the girls were whispering about Steve. *(Pause for girls' actions)* Some said he was gay; *(Pause for girls' actions)* others said he was just stupid. *(Pause for girls' actions)* The guys all laughed at him. *(Pause for guys' actions)* Steve felt like crawling into a hole, *(Pause for Steve's actions)* but he knew he'd done the right thing.

Meanwhile, Denise picked out a certain special guy from among the other guys. *(Pause for Denise's and guy's actions)* They dated for several months, too. Then Denise's boyfriend asked for her rose. At first she refused. *(Pause for Denise's and guy's actions)* But he seemed so hurt and sad that she felt sorry for him. *(Pause for Denise's and guy's actions)* "After all," she thought, "he loves me, and we'll probably get married someday." So she gave him her rose. *(Pause for Denise's and guy's actions)*

He took the rose out of the box and accidently bent the stem. *(Pause for guy's actions)* Before long, all he cared about was Denise's rose. He rarely talked with her anymore. They broke up during their senior year because the guy found someone new. *(Pause for Denise's and guy's actions)*

In time, other guys asked for Denise's rose, too. *(Pause for Denise's and guys' actions)* Some pulled off a few petals. *(Pause for guys' actions)* A few more bent the stem. *(Pause for guys' actions)* Time passed, and Denise began to long for her rose to be new like it once was. But try as she might, she couldn't get her rose to look as it had when God gave it to her. *(Pause for Denise's actions)*

Then she started going out with Steve. *(Pause for Steve's and Denise's actions)* They dated for some time, but Steve never asked for her rose, even though she expected him to. Finally the day came when they walked down the aisle to be married. *(Pause for Steve's and Denise's actions)*

For a wedding present, Steve gave Denise his rose *(Pause for Steve's and Denise's actions)* and was proud he'd kept it in such good condition for her.

How do you think Denise felt when she gave Steve her rose?

BEFORE THE FINAL CURTAIN

Have kids read Romans 6:12-14 and Ephesians 5:1-3 and discuss these questions.
1. How would you have felt if you'd been Steve? if you'd been Denise?
2. Why do you think Romans 6:12-14 and Ephesians 5:1-3 discourage sex before marriage? What's your opinion on sex before marriage?
3. In what ways do guys and girls pressure each other into having sex? In what ways can guys and girls can encourage each other to save sex for marriage?
4. How can a person who's already had sexual relations restore his or her "rose"? Read 2 Corinthians 5:17. How can God restore a person's rose?

AFTER THE SHOW

Try these activities for further study.
1. Have kids discuss the dangers of being sexually active. Encourage kids to think through consequences such as the risk of pregnancy and early parenthood, AIDS and other sexually transmitted diseases, loss of one's reputation, shame and inability to forgive oneself, and a hampered relationship with God.

2. Go for a nature walk in a nearby park or wilderness area. Have kids look for ways humans have treated God's creation carelessly with litter or lack of proper care. Then discuss the importance of caring for God's creation of sexuality. Compare rewards of caring for creation to rewards of being careful with our sexuality.

Opening Night

Theme:

RACISM AND
PREJUDICE

Scripture:

COLOSSIANS
3:10-15

The freedom marches of the 1960s are over, but racism and prejudice live on. No longer simply an issue of white vs. black, racism occurs in every culture and at every level of society. Rich, poor, African-American, Caucasian, Hispanic, Asian, Middle-Eastern, young, old, rural, and urban; everyone in this list is guilty of prejudice at some level.

Junior highers are especially vulnerable to making judgments about people on the basis of outward appearances. Many of your group members may also be victims of unfair bias.

Use this skit to help kids win their struggles with racism and prejudice.

PROPS

For this skit you'll need

- some kind of food everyone in your group will like. It can be a big bowl of popcorn, candy, doughnuts, cookies, or even pizza. You'll need enough for everyone in the group.

SETTING THE STAGE

Before the meeting, read the entire skit at least once to become familiar with the story. Also, section off an area of the room to be the club in the skit. You can use chairs, tables, or even masking tape on the floor. Be sure to include a door for your club.

This skit has a number of "fill in the blank" spaces. Involve the entire group in filling in these blanks before you begin the performance. To do this, read the descriptions under each blank and have kids suggest words or phrases to fill in the blank. Write kids' suggestions in pencil in the blanks. Don't give any further information about the skit while kids are making suggestions.

Form the following groups:
Group 1.......... Everyone born during winter (December, January, February)
Group 2.......... Everyone born during spring (March, April, May)

Group 3.......... Everyone born during summer (June, July, August)
Group 4.......... Everyone born during fall (September, October, November)

Inform students that as you read the skit *Opening Night*, you'll point to one or more groups to perform actions illustrating the skit. For example, if the skit says, "There were a couple of basketballs," have kids bounce up and down to imitate a basketball. Encourage kids to be creative and to work as a team during the performance. You'll be prompted during the skit as to which group or groups to point to.

The ending of this skit is intentionally left incomplete. When you get to the end, be prepared to direct groups to come up with their own endings.

THE PERFORMANCE:
Opening Night

There was once a place called _____ . Not much
name of a local school
happened there until a company came in and decided to convert it into a new club just for junior highers. It was going to be called

_____ , and people would _____ , *(Point*
name of a breakfast cereal   *verb*

to group 1) _____ , *(Point to group 2)* _____ ,
verb   *verb*

(Point to group 3) and _____ *(Point to group 4)* there
verb

every night. And just as importantly, there would be no

_____ . *(Point to all groups)*
activity you hate to do

The club was really _____ . *(Point to group 3)* There was
adjective

a _____ . *(Point to group 1)* And nearby, there
something you might find at a dance

was _____ . *(Point to group 4)* There were
something you might find at a ski lodge

a couple of _____ . *(Point to*
something you could buy at a sporting goods store

group 2) And people were _____ .
something you would see people doing at a wedding

(Point to group 2)

On opening night, everyone got into their _____ ,
form of transportation

(Point to all groups) and went to pick up their dates for the evening. *(Point to all groups)* After picking up their dates, everyone showed up to have a great time. Most people were busy introducing their dates to one another *(Point to all groups)* and learning favorite pizza toppings of three other people. *(Point to all groups)*

At one end of the club, people were having a great time
_____ . *(Point to group 4)* On the dance floor people
    verb that ends with "-ing".

were _____ . *(Point to group 1)* Outside everyone was
    verb that ends with "-ing".

_____ . *(Point to group 2)* And everywhere inside
    verb that ends with "-ing".

the club, you could hear people _____ . *(Point to*
                    verb that ends with "-ing".

group 3)

Halfway into the evening _____ got up to per-
               name of a music group

form. Their first song was _____ , and they
           name of a song

performed it loudly. *(Point to group 1)* The crowd went _____ .
                                      adjective

(Point to group 3) Then a _____ contest began on
                  noun—not a proper name

the dance floor between people born in spring and people born in

fall. *(Point to groups 2 and 4)* When it was over, there was

applause for everyone. *(Point to all groups)*

Just when things were getting fun, _____ jumped
                                one of the youth leaders

onstage to make an announcement. *(Point to group 2)*

"There seems to have been a misunderstanding. Some undesir-

ables have accidentally gotten into the club. If your birthday is

during the summer months, you must now leave." *(Point to group*

3 and send them "out" through the "door")

To make sure the summer people couldn't get back in, the

_____ stationed bouncers at the door. *(Point to group 1)*
    same youth leader

Then, _____ brought out food only for those who
        same youth leader

were allowed to stay at the club. *(Bring out food for the group)*

There was plenty to go around, and those left at the club enjoyed

every bite. *(Point to groups 1, 2, and 4)*

What did everyone else do? Well, what would you do?

(At this point, have students from group 3 rejoin the other groups
and allow them to enjoy the food.

Then have each group write an ending to the skit. Encourage them
to decide what they would actually do about the unfair way group 3

was treated. Some may decide to do nothing. Others might take some form of action, such as a loud protest or trying to force group 3's return to the club.

Have groups take turns leading everyone in performing their endings.)

BEFORE THE FINAL CURTAIN

Have kids read Colossians 3:10-15 and discuss these questions.

1. How did you feel when group 3 was forced to leave? Why?
2. How was this skit an example of racism or prejudice? What would be an example of Colossians 3:10-15 in action?
3. What does Colossians 3:10-15 say about God's attitude toward racism and prejudice? What's your attitude about racism and prejudice?
4. How do you respond when you or someone you know is treated unfairly on the basis of race, religious beliefs, financial status, or social status? How would Jesus respond?

AFTER THE SHOW

Try these activities for further study.

1. Invite a foreign exchange student or a missionary from another country to visit your group. Encourage your students to ask plenty of questions about your visitor's experiences. Then, as a group, brainstorm and implement ways to show support for these people.
2. Have a taste test using a large bag of jelly beans. Let students pick their favorite flavors and discuss what it would be like if only one flavor were available.

Ask questions such as, **"Is there such a thing as a 'right' or 'wrong' flavor?"** and **"How would our world be different if God had created only one 'flavor' or nationality of people?"**

Ruined by Rumor

Theme:
GOSSIP

Scripture:
JAMES 3:3-12

It started out innocently enough. Sara saw Tia at the movies with a guy who definitely wasn't Tia's boyfriend, Shawn. So Sara called Shawn and a few other people to let them know. Later, she found out that the guy was Tia's brother, home from college for the weekend.

Like Sara, most junior highers are vulnerable to the double-edged sword of gossip. A word here, a nod there, and suddenly the whole school is spreading rumors. Use this skit to help students discover the lasting damage gossip can do.

PROPS

For this skit you'll need

- a bag of marshmallows and
- a clean floor.

SETTING THE STAGE

Before the meeting, read the entire skit at least once to become familiar with the story.

Form three groups and assign groups the following roles:

Group 1 ....Rumor-Mouth Ralph
Group 2 ....Wise One
Group 3 ....Rumor Vultures

Say: **As I read the skit** *Ruined by Rumor,* **think of actions to illustrate the story. When I pause during the story, that'll be your cue to act out your group's part in the skit. Be creative and have fun with this.**

Encourage kids to react dramatically to what you read. Watch for the pause prompts as you read and allow time for students to perform their actions before continuing with the story. Read with exaggerated expression so it will be easier for the kids to showcase their melodramatic talents!

THE PERFORMANCE:
Ruined by Rumor

Rumor-Mouth Ralph was troubled. He shook his head wildly, *(Pause for Ralph's actions)* jumped up and down, *(Pause for Ralph's actions)* and moaned, "There must be a way to take it back! There must be way to stop this RUMOR!" *(Pause for Ralph's actions)*

In the distance, Rumor-Mouth Ralph could hear the Rumor Vultures cackling loudly as they devoured another rumor. *(Pause for Ralph's and Vultures' actions)*

Finally Rumor-Mouth Ralph smacked his head, *(Pause for Ralph's actions)* opened his eyes wide, *(Pause for Ralph's actions)* and said, "I know exactly what to do!"

And Rumor-Mouth Ralph ran off to find the Wise One. *(Pause for Ralph's actions)* Rumor-Mouth Ralph was out of breath when he finally found the Wise One in an old corn field. *(Pause for Ralph's actions)*

The Wise One sat on the ground with her legs crossed and her head in her hands, *(Pause for Wise One's actions)* snoring loudly. *(Pause for Wise One's actions)*

Rumor-Mouth Ralph shook the Wise One *(Pause for Ralph's actions)* and cried, "You must help me! You're my only hope!" *(Pause for Ralph's actions)*

The Wise One rubbed her eyes and yawned loudly. *(Pause for Wise One's actions)* Stretching, *(Pause for Wise One's actions)* she grumbled, "What do you want?"

"I've made a terrible mistake. I started a rumor, and now everyone believes it," Rumor-Mouth Ralph sniffed as he cried on the Wise One's shoulder. *(Pause for Ralph's actions)* Rumor-Mouth Ralph shook the Wise One's arm and said, "Please, you have to help me undo my rumor!" *(Pause for Ralph's actions)*

Just then a flock of Rumor Vultures flew by. *(Pause for Vultures' actions)* When they saw Rumor-Mouth Ralph, they turned around and flew circles around him in hopes that he might toss them more rumors. *(Pause for Vultures' actions)* But he just shooed them away, *(Pause for Ralph's actions)* so they returned to their nests. *(Pause for Vultures' actions)*

The Wise One slowly got up, cracked her knuckles, *(Pause for Wise One's actions)* and said, "Rumors are nasty things. However, if you do what I tell you, the rumor will be gone."

Rumor-Mouth Ralph nodded vigorously and hugged the Wise One's ankle in appreciation. *(Pause for Ralph's actions)* The Wise One handed Rumor-Mouth Ralph a bag of marshmallows. *(Pause for Wise One's actions)*

"Take these marshmallows and spread them on the path to town," the Wise One said. "Then tomorrow morning, go back to the path and pick up each and every piece. When the last piece is in the bag, the rumor will have vanished."

Rumor-Mouth Ralph gleefully spread the marshmallows all over the path to town. *(Pause for Ralph's actions)* When he was finished, he crawled home—exhausted. *(Pause for Ralph's actions)* At home, Rumor-Mouth Ralph climbed into bed, pulled his covers up, closed his eyes, and began to snore loudly. *(Pause for Ralph's actions)*

As the sun set, a flock of Rumor Vultures flew through the sky hunting for food. *(Pause for Vultures' actions)* When they saw the marshmallows on the path, the Rumor Vultures flapped their wings wildly *(Pause for Vultures' actions)* and dove for the sweet treats. Greedily, the birds gulped down every marshmallow *(Pause for Vultures' actions)* and waddled home—too fat to fly. *(Pause for Vultures' actions)*

Rumor-Mouth Ralph awoke in the morning, rubbing his tired, sore muscles. *(Pause for Ralph's actions)* He grabbed the marshmallow bag and started slowly out the door, *(Pause for Ralph's actions)* grateful that today his troubles would be over and the rumor would be history. Step by step, he stumbled quickly to the path where he had left the marshmallows the night before. *(Pause for Ralph's actions)*

But when he got there, the marshmallows were gone. Rumor-Mouth Ralph looked everywhere, his eyes opened wide in shock and disbelief. *(Pause for Ralph's actions)* Finally he gave up, knelt on the bare ground, and threw a tantrum. *(Pause for Ralph's actions)*

That's where the Wise One found him. *(Pause for Wise One's actions)* She knelt beside Rumor-Mouth Ralph *(Pause for Wise One's actions)* and gently said, "Rumors are practically impossible to stop, and once they've started, the Rumor Vultures eat them up and fly them to parts unknown. The only real way to stop a rumor is to not start it."

And the Rumor Vultures cackled hungrily once more. *(Pause for Vultures' actions)*

BEFORE THE FINAL CURTAIN

Have kids read James 3:3-12 and discuss these questions.

1. How was James 3:3-12 illustrated in this skit? How would you have felt if you'd been in Rumor-Mouth Ralph's situation? if you were the person Rumor-Mouth Ralph's rumor was about?

2. How do you respond when people spread rumors about you? What are some positive responses to gossip?

3. How would you summarize James 3:3-12 in eight words or less? How can we encourage each other to follow the advice of James this week?

AFTER THE SHOW

Try these activities for further study.

1. Form six groups (a group can be one person). Assign each group one of the following scriptures: Proverbs 11:13; 16:28; 18:8; 26:20; Ephesians 4:29; and James 1:26. If you have fewer than six students, form three groups and assign each group two scriptures.

Give each group a sheet of newsprint and a marker. Instruct them to each create a comic strip that illustrates the main point of their scripture. Tell kids stick figures are acceptable.

Have the groups share their comic strips with one another and then discuss how they can "illustrate" these scriptures in their daily lives.

2. Have a Tabloid-Rumors Scavenger Hunt. Buy five copies of a supermarket tabloid and bring them to your youth group meeting. Form four groups and give each group one copy of the tabloid. Have groups split pages of the tabloid evenly among their members.

Then, using the fifth copy of the tabloid, look for words, titles, or pictures for the groups to search for. For example, you might call out, "I'm looking for a picture of a space alien with the president." Award points to the first group whose representative can find the picture and show it to you.

Afterward, discuss how to avoid the temptation to search for gossip and spread untrue rumors.

Ronnie Raindrop's Remarkable Journey

Theme:

ANXIETY AND FEAR

Scripture:

MATTHEW 6:25-34 AND PHILIPPIANS 4:6-7

Ever play the game "What If?" That's the game where you imagine what life would be like if circumstances were different. What if you were a prince or princess? a world famous athlete? a movie star?

For junior highers, "What If?" often takes a more serious turn. What if my parents get a divorce? What if I flunk this class? What if I'm the victim of gang violence?

Kids need to learn that Jesus has all the answers to life's "what ifs." Use this skit to help your kids turn to Jesus for help in dealing with anxiety and fear.

PROPS

No props are needed for this skit.

SETTING THE STAGE

Before the meeting, read the entire skit at least once to become familiar with the story.

Say: **Close your eyes for a moment and imagine what it might be like to be a raindrop. How might you feel?**

Allow a few students respond. Then form groups of no more than five and say: **Let's do a group skit called** *Ronnie Raindrop's Remarkable Journey* **and experience what it might be like to be a raindrop. As I read the skit, I'll pause after "feeling" words such as anger, happiness, and amazement. That'll be your group's cue to create a group statue that illustrates that emotion.**

For example, if I read the word "anger," you might form a circle with one group member in the middle and have the rest of the group pose as people who are about to hit him or her. When I pause, you'll have 30 seconds to form your statues and freeze. Stay frozen until the next pause. Ready? Let's have some fun!

Read the skit, taking care to pause at the italicized words. Read with enthusiasm and applaud your students' enthusiasm as well.

THE PERFORMANCE:
Ronnie Raindrop's Remarkable Journey

It was a day just like any other day. Ronnie Raindrop was snuggled in his feather bed, feeling *CONTENTED*. He wiggled and shimmered as he pulled the covers closer, closing his eyes to block out the morning sun.

Suddenly, he heard sounds of laughter floating between the thin walls of his cloud and knew that his friends and family were already out of bed.

"I wonder what they're up to," he thought. "How could they start having fun without me?" Feeling *EXCLUDED*, he trudged down the long hallway, until he could hear the laughter only inches away. *ENVIOUSLY*, he peeked around the corner and, to his *AMAZEMENT*, the Master of the cloud was holding a meeting.

"Ronnie," he said, "We've been waiting for you. Have a seat and we'll begin."

A little *CONFUSED*, Ronnie Raindrop found a seat.

The Master of the cloud spoke, "Today I'm sending you out on a dangerous mission. The earth below us is in desperate need of water, and so you must rain down on it and restore its strength. Some of you may not finish your journey or may be swept away by rivers and streams. But have no *FEAR*, because I'll be with you no matter where you go. Prepare to depart."

And with that, the Master dismissed the meeting. The raindrops scurried around, talking *EXCITEDLY* and getting ready for the Big Drop. But Ronnie had never been away from the cloud before, and he was *NERVOUS*.

Finally everyone was ready. They gathered in the meeting room and faced the Master as he spoke a blessing for them. Then it happened. The floor moved. Ronnie Raindrop heard an awful sound. Loud and low, it sounded as if the cloud were groaning. Shaking with *FRIGHT*, Ronnie Raindrop and his friends fell silent. Suddenly, the bottom of the cloud ripped open. Ronnie and the other raindrops tumbled toward earth like a million tiny missiles.

Ronnie Raindrop's mouth opened in *DISBELIEF*. He was so *SAD* because he knew that after today his life would never be the same. Though his friends surrounded him, Ronnie Raindrop felt more *ALONE* than he had ever felt before. He longed for the safety of the cloud and the *LOVING* Master who ruled it.

He closed his eyes tightly, *MISERABLE* and *DEPRESSED*. Ronnie didn't want to fall to the ground. He was *SCARED*. And then he heard a voice, faint at first, barely audible above the roar of the wind.

"Don't be *AFRAID*. I've come to bring you *PEACE*." Ronnie Raindrop squinted one eye open as he continued to fall. Where was the whisper coming from? He strained his ears to listen, desperately wanting to *TRUST* the sound of the voice.

And then he heard it again. "Don't be *AFRAID*. I am with you always." This time he could feel warmth in the voice. With great caution, he slowly opened his eyes and saw the Spirit of the Master beside him.

Feelings of *RELIEF, LOVE,* and *JOY* washed over Ronnie. And his eyes were opened to see the beauty of the world around him. Ronnie Raindrop continued his descent to earth, *AMAZED* at the sights to be seen: giant trees, bright birds, granite buildings, and funny little people running on skinny legs, with big cups upside down over their heads. Ronnie Raindrop even began to look with *ANTICIPATION* to his destination.

Moments later, Ronnie Raindrop splashed deeply into the earth.

After a few days, Ronnie Raindrop heard a familiar voice. The Master of the cloud spoke. "Well done, my good and faithful servant. It's time to come home." In the twinkling of an eye, an *ASTONISHED* Ronnie Raindrop evaporated back to his *PEACEFUL* cloud.

The smile on the Master's face was the greatest reward Ronnie Raindrop could ever have asked for. Ronnie Raindrop went to bed that night *SATISFIED* he'd completed a job well done.

BEFORE THE FINAL CURTAIN

Have kids read Matthew 6:25-34 and Philippians 4:6-7 and discuss these questions.

1. How would you have felt if you had been in Ronnie Raindrop's situation? What real-life situations cause you to feel the emotions Ronnie Raindrop did?
2. How was this skit an illustration of Matthew 6:25-34 and Philippians 4:6-7? Do you find it easy or difficult to apply these scriptures to your life on a daily basis? Explain.
3. What do you do when you're feeling afraid or worried? What advice would you give a friend who was feeling scared or anxious?
4. When is fear or anxiety a healthy feeling? Explain. When is fear or anxiety unhealthy? Explain.

AFTER THE SHOW

Try these activities for further study.

1. Take your group for a visit to the snake exhibit at the zoo. While inside the darkened corridors, have kids discuss their feelings about snakes. Help kids discover which snakes are dangerous and which are harmless. Likewise, encourage kids to assess the things that scare them and determine which are really dangerous and which are actually harmless. Then compare methods for subduing snakes to methods for subduing fears.

2. Have your kids create an "Anxiety Attack Pack." Give each person a paper bag with instructions to fill it with objects to help them deal with anxious feelings. Start off their kits by putting some of the following things in the bags:
   - a 3×5 card with Philippians 4:6-7 written on it,
   - a Rolodex card with a space to put the phone number of a friend or the church on it, and
   - a chocolate bar!

A Star Goes Afar

Theme:

GOD'S LOVE

Scripture:

LUKE 15:3-7

"I *blew it again," says Melissa. "Now everyone will hate me. How can I ever face my parents again?"*

As she starts to cry, Melissa wonders why she strayed from what she knew was right. She feels worthless and afraid, much like a sheep that has been separated from its flock.

But like a little, lost lamb, Melissa is being pursued by a caring shepherd—a shepherd who can and will bring her back to the safety of the flock. That shepherd is God.

Use this intergalactic skit to help kids understand God's persevering love is reaching out for them.

PROPS

For this skit you'll need

- six photocopies of the "Create a Character" handout and
- six rolls of tinfoil.

SETTING THE STAGE

Before the meeting, read the entire skit at least once to become familiar with the story.

Form six groups (a group can be one person) and assign each group the following roles:

Group 1	Master Monga
Group 2	Monga Bunga Monsters
Group 3	Bunga Buggy
Group 4	Star Streamer Beamer
Group 5	Purple Suction Maze
Group 6	Super-Sonic Spitter Star

Give each group a photocopy of the "Create a Character" handout and a roll of tinfoil. Allow groups time to create their characters and to put together tinfoil props and costumes.

After groups have decided on sounds and actions for their characters and are suitably dressed, have everyone practice their responses before you read the story.

When groups are ready, read aloud the skit *A Star Goes Afar*. Pause for group responses each time you see an italicized word. Don't worry if the actions your kids perform are inconsistent with the story. That will just make an absurd story even funnier. Applaud wild creativity and encourage the kids to be as dramatic as possible when performing.

THE PERFORMANCE:
A Star Goes Afar

Long ago, in a galaxy far away, there lived a people who called themselves *MONGA BUNGA MONSTERS*. As was their custom, they all worked busily to prepare for the annual space expedition. Once each year, the *MASTER MONGA* and *MONGA BUNGA MONSTERS* polished their *BUNGA BUGGY,* loaded the massive *STAR STREAMER BEAMER,* and set out to clean the *SUPER-SONIC SPITTER STARS* before the stars grew rusty, blew their fuses, and faded into nothingness.

This expedition was dangerous because star checking was continually thwarted by the ugly and vicious *PURPLE SUCTION MAZE,* which took great delight in sucking in a *BUNGA BUGGY* for dinner. But the *MASTER MONGA* was the best star checker of them all.

The *MASTER MONGA* carefully looked over the space charts, plotting and graphing and noting the latest sightings of the *PURPLE SUCTION MAZE*. The *MONGA BUNGA MONSTERS* applied an extra layer of stealth to the *STAR STREAMER BEAMER*. Then the *MASTER MONGA* called the *MONGA BUNGA MONSTERS* to their *BUNGA BUGGY* and gave the take-off order.

The first few days were without incident. The *STAR STREAMER BEAMER* had great success in cleaning the *SUPER-SONIC SPITTER STARS*. But on the fourth day, a small, impish *SUPER-SONIC SPITTER STAR* decided to return home and skip its cleaning. Without alerting the *MONGA BUNGA MONSTERS*, this little *SUPER-SONIC SPITTER STAR* let go of the *STAR STREAMER BEAMER* and floated quietly away.

Now the *MONGA BUNGA MONSTERS* always counted their stars each hour. At last count, there had been 100, and the *MONGA BUNGA MONSTERS* fully expected that this hour would yield the same results. One, two, three, four... 97, 98, 99.

Where was 100? *SUPER-SONIC SPITTER STARS* didn't just disappear. Not with the *MASTER MONGA* in charge. They counted again. Still only 99. Where had that star gone?

They didn't know it, but the missing *SUPER-SONIC SPITTER STAR* was in serious trouble. Lost, frightened, and alone, the star wished it hadn't been so quick to leave. Home was still out of reach for the tiring star, and the *BUNGA BUGGY* was long out of sight. Before long, the *PURPLE SUCTION MAZE* swallowed it whole.

Back on the *BUNGA BUGGY*, the *MASTER MONGA* and the *MONGA BUNGA MONSTERS* couldn't believe a *SUPER-SONIC SPITTER STAR* had disappeared. The *STAR STREAMER BEAMER* had always held onto the stars tightly before. The *MASTER MONGA* gave the order to turn the *BUNGA BUGGY* around.

Some *MONGA BUNGA MONSTERS* protested, "It's only one star, one small, tiny star. We have 99 others. Turning back is too dangerous. We're almost home, safe from the *PURPLE SUC-TION MAZE*. Don't go back! It's useless!"

But it was no use complaining. The *MASTER MONGA* cared for all the stars. The *BUNGA BUGGY* turned around and began the long search for the lost *SUPER-SONIC SPITTER STAR* .

Finally, the *STAR STREAMER BEAMER* locked onto a small, faint light in space. But the blinking light was enveloped by purple patches, the dreaded sign of a nearby *PURPLE SUCTION MAZE*.

Again the *PURPLE SUCTION MAZE* opened its jaws, and the *MASTER MONGA* saw the blinking light. The *MONGA BUNGA MONSTERS* shot a line from the *STAR STREAMER BEAMER* straight into the mouth of the *PURPLE SUCTION MAZE* and hooked the *SUPER-SONIC SPITTER STAR*. Quickly, the *BUNGA BUGGY* violently reversed its motion, pulling the star out of reach of the *PURPLE SUCTION MAZE*.

The rest of the journey home was uneventful. The wayward *SUPER-SONIC SPITTER STAR* was forever thankful, and upon returning home, a huge crowd cheered the *MONGA BUNGA MONSTERS'* brave and unselfish act.

Sometimes, if the astral winds are just right, you can still hear echoes of the universe-sized party they held to celebrate the return of the *SUPER-SONIC SPITTER STAR*.

BEFORE THE FINAL CURTAIN

Have groups read Luke 15:3-7 and discuss these questions. Tell groups to select two representatives to share their answers with everyone else.

1. How did you feel during the skit? Explain.

2. How are the skit *A Star Goes Afar* and the parable of the lost sheep in Luke 15:3-7 similar to real life?

3. The Super-Sonic Spitter Star turned its back on the Master Monga and was forgiven. How do you think God reacts when you turn your back on him?

4. Do you think God loves you enough to forgive you? Why or why not? How does that affect the way you live?

AFTER THE SHOW

Try these activities for further study.

1. Bring a star map to your youth meeting (check your local library for one). Allow kids to examine and quiz one another on their knowledge of the stars.

Then have kids complete this sentence about themselves: "One way I'm a star in God's eyes is . . . "

2. Visit a petting zoo. Have kids pay particular attention to the sheep they see. Form trios and have each trio write five things they observe about sheep.

Gather the group together and discuss the observations the kids made. Then have kids compare themselves to the sheep. How are they alike? different? What can junior highers learn from sheep?

End the trip with a sheep imitation contest and have kids bleat their best "baaas" all the way home.

Create a Character

Your group will be acting out one of the unique characters in the skit A Star Goes Afar. After you get your role assignment, take a few moments to create a personality and some sounds and actions to describe your character. Whenever you hear the name of your character mentioned during the skit, perform your sounds and actions. Make sure your actions include every person in your group.

Use these questions to help form your character:
- Exactly what is your character?
- What are your character's likes and dislikes?
- What actions can your group do that will communicate your character's personality to the rest of the group? Think of three or four and use them at different times during the skit.

The Day of the Pimple

*"**I**mage is everything. It doesn't matter who you are as long as you look like who you want to be. If you want to be loved, you've got to look lovely."*

These are the spoken and unspoken messages junior highers hear about life. And so they struggle to look just right, to act "cool," and to fit in. They need to discover the news that God doesn't base his love on outward appearances. Use this skit to help your kids understand God loves them, no matter what.

Theme:
SELF-IMAGE

Scripture:
ROMANS 8:35-39

PROPS

No props are needed for this skit.

SETTING THE STAGE

Before the meeting, read the entire skit at least once to become familiar with the story.

Form groups of no more than five and have kids number off from one to five within each group. Assign group members the following roles:

Ones	Jill
Twos	Jill's mother
Threes	Todd, Jill's little brother
Fours	Ryan
Fives	Beth, Ryan's little sister

If you have a group of fewer than five, have kids play more than one role.

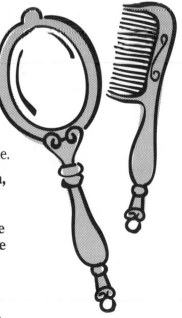

Say: **We're going to perform an episode of the newest soap opera,** *The Day of the Pimple.* **In your group form a circle. As I read the script for the soap opera, think of actions to illustrate the story. When I pause during the story, that'll be your cue to move to the center of your circle and act out your part in the skit. Be creative and have fun with this.**

Encourage kids to exaggerate their actions dramatically. Watch for the pause prompts as you read and allow time for kids to perform their actions before continuing with the story. Read with soap opera-ish melodrama to set the tone for the skit. And have fun!

THE PERFORMANCE:
The Day of the Pimple

The day of the big school dance finally arrived, and students at Roosevelt High School made frenzied preparations for the big event. One student, Jill, was particularly frantic.

Jill paced the floor in her bedroom and twirled her hair, trying to get ready for the dance. *(Pause for Jill's actions)* There was a knock on the door. *(Pause and make a knocking sound)* Jill opened the door, grabbed her mother, and whined, "I'll never be ready!" *(Pause for Jill's actions)* Jill's mother held her hands over her ears and shook her head as she surveyed the disaster in Jill's room. *(Pause for mother's actions)*

"What's going on in here?" Jill's mother asked. "What a mess!" She walked to the bed and picked up one hanger after another. *(Pause for mother's actions)*

Jill fell on the bed, covered her eyes, and sobbed. *(Pause for Jill's actions)* "Nothing looks right on me. I hate my clothes. Where's my red outfit, anyway?"

Jill's mother sat on the bed and put her arm around Jill to comfort her. *(Pause for mother's actions)* "It's in the wash. Why don't you wear the green one?" she suggested.

Jill rushed to the mirror, pressed her face against it, tugged her hair, and screeched. *(Pause for Jill's actions)* "Green looks awful with my hair. It makes me look like I'm dead and decaying." Jill fell back onto the bed and played dead. *(Pause for Jill's actions)*

Loud banging echoed through the room. *(Pause and bang on floor)* Jill's little brother was on the other side, kicking and thumping on the door. *(Pause for Todd's actions)*

Jill started crying—again. *(Pause for Jill's actions)* Her little brother, Todd, raced into the room, shook her shoulders, and yelled, "Wake up! Ryan's on the phone. I told him you were busy trying to get the bats out of your hair." *(Pause for Todd's actions)*

Jill pushed her brother away and ran out screaming, "I hate you! Why did God give me such a rotten little brother?" *(Pause for Jill's actions)*

Jill's mother grabbed Todd by his shirt *(Pause for mother's actions)* and said, "Leave her alone. Now go on outside and play." Todd stuck out his tongue, laughed, and hopped out of the room.

(Pause for Todd's actions) Jill's mother sighed and held her hands on her head. *(Pause for mother's actions)*

Jill picked up the phone and said, "H-i-i-i, Ryan! It's so sw-e-e-e-t of you to call." *(Pause for Jill's actions)* She giggled a few times, smiled, and then blew a kiss into the phone. *(Pause for Jill's actions)* She hung up and skipped lightly to her room, smiling. *(Pause for Jill's actions)* Jill grabbed her mother, spun her around and sang, "He likes me, he likes me, he likes me. He said I was beautiful." *(Pause for Jill's actions)* Jill folded her hands, looked up, and whispered, "Thank you, God." *(Pause for Jill's actions)*

Meanwhile, Jill's date, Ryan, bent over the bathroom sink and washed his face. He closed his eyes tightly and hummed to himself. *(Pause for Ryan's actions)* As he splashed water on his face, Ryan heard a knock on the door. *(Pause and make a knocking sound)*

Squinting one eye open, Ryan said, "Come in." *(Pause for Ryan's actions)* The door opened, and Ryan's little sister, Beth, bounced into the room. *(Pause for Beth's actions)* She held her hands over her mouth and giggled loudly. *(Pause for Beth's actions)*

"Are you going to kiss her tonight? Yuck! No boy will ever get his germs on me!" she taunted. *(Pause for Beth's actions)* She made a goofy face at Ryan, puckered up her lips, kissed the air, and ran out of the room. *(Pause for Beth's actions)*

Ryan slammed the door shut and locked it. *(Pause for Ryan's actions)* He dressed, carefully combed his hair, and brushed his teeth. *(Pause for Ryan's actions)* Looking in the mirror and flexing his muscles, he gave the "thumbs up" sign to his reflection. *(Pause for Ryan's actions)*

Back at her home, Jill, too, was in the bathroom, spraying every last hair to keep it all in place. *(Pause for Jill's actions)* She flossed her teeth, checked for zits, and doused herself with perfume. *(Pause for Jill's actions)* One last inspection in the mirror, and she gave herself a great big smile. "I am gorgeous," she whispered to her reflection and danced out the bathroom door. *(Pause for Jill's actions)*

Twenty minutes later, the doorbell rang. Jill raced down the hall to look at herself one more time in the bedroom mirror. *(Pause for Jill's actions)* Jill's brother stopped playing ball and ran to the door to see what Ryan looked like. He tripped over the front step and fell on Ryan, knocking him down. *(Pause for Todd's and Ryan's actions)*

Jill's mother opened the door and saw Ryan and Todd on the ground. Both were struggling to get up. *(Pause for Todd's and Ryan's actions)*

Meanwhile, Jill looked at herself in the mirror. Her eyes opened wide. *(Pause for Jill's actions)* She pressed her face against the mirror and touched the tip of her nose with her finger. *(Pause for Jill's actions)* A huge pimple was starting to grow! *(Pause for Jill's actions)*

Jill screamed. *(Pause for Jill's actions)* Ryan and Todd fell down again. *(Pause for Todd's and Ryan's actions)* Jill's mother covered her ears and ran to the bedroom. She found Jill shaking her fists and screaming. *(Pause for Jill's actions)*

Jill said sadly, "How can I go out in public with a pimple on my nose? Everyone will laugh at me. What's the use? I'm worthless." She slumped onto her bed. *(Pause for Jill's actions)*

Ryan shook his head and walked out. *(Pause for Ryan's actions)* Jill's mother tried to comfort Jill. *(Pause for mother's actions)* Todd just laughed. *(Pause for Todd's actions)*

When Ryan got home, he took his sister out for ice cream instead of going to the dance. *(Pause for Ryan's and Beth's actions)* Beth didn't care what she looked like—even when she had chocolate ice cream smeared on her cheek.

And neither did God.

BEFORE THE FINAL CURTAIN

Have kids read Romans 8:35-39 and discuss these questions.

1. What message should Jill hear from Romans 8:35-39? On what things is she basing her self-worth? How does God determine a person's worth?
2. How would you have reacted in Jill's position? in Ryan's? How do you think God would want you to react?
3. When have you felt like Jill? How can Romans 8:35-39 help you deal with those times? How can you encourage others with the message of Romans 8:35-39?

AFTER THE SHOW

Try these activities for further study.

1. Give each group member a sheet of paper and make colored markers available to all kids. Then have kids each make a miniature billboard based on the theme "Nothing can separate me from the love of Jesus." Encourage kids to use creative images or words on their billboards. Afterward, tell kids to take their billboards home and hang them on their mirrors as a daily reminder of God's loving acceptance.

2. Have a pass-the-lemon affirmation time. Form a circle and give one person a lemon. Tell that person one positive quality you see in him or her, such as a friendly smile or helpful attitude. Then have that person pass the lemon to someone else in the circle and do the same thing. Continue passing the lemon until everyone has had an opportunity to be affirmed. Then take out a bag of lemons, a lemon squeezer, sugar, and water and lead the group in making a big pitcher of lemonade!

The Super Race

Theme:

DREAMS AND GOALS

Scripture:

PHILIPPIANS 3:12-14

"When I finish high school, I want to go to an Ivy League college."

"Someday I'll be a world famous writer."

"Wouldn't it be great if I were drafted by the Phoenix Suns?"

For many junior highers, the hope of achieving a dream is dimmed by the harsh realities of life. Junior highers often feel too young, too ugly, too dumb, or too clumsy to accomplish lofty goals. But where would we be if Edison had quit dreaming about the light bulb? if Churchill had abandoned the goal of defeating Hitler? if God had given up on his creation?

Use this skit to show junior highers the value of dreams and goals. Help them understand the powerful role Jesus can play in setting and achieving goals—and in overcoming failures.

PROPS

For this skit you'll need

● enough snacks and drinks for everyone in the group. Use these for the victory celebration at the end of the skit.

SETTING THE STAGE

Before the meeting, read the entire skit at least once to become familiar with the story.

Form up to 12 teams based on group members' birth months. For example, all kids born in January form one team, all kids born in February form another, and so on. A team can be one person, and it's okay if some months aren't represented. However, if you have fewer than six months represented, form six teams and assign each team a month of the year.

Have teams take a few minutes to create a cheer. Remind kids that cheers should be positive and put-downs aren't acceptable. When teams are ready, have kids practice their cheers once before starting the skit.

Then say: **For this skit, each of the teams will act as a contestant in the race to end all races—the Super Race! When I pause during the story, that'll be your team's cue to perform the actions in the skit. Be creative and have fun. Now, let the race begin!**

Read the skit enthusiastically, pausing where indicated to allow teams to perform their actions.

THE PERFORMANCE:
The Super Race

The air was chilly, and emotion was high as contestants gathered for the Ninth Annual Super Race—the race to end all races. Everyone dreamed of competing in this race, but only one team would reach the ultimate goal—to win the race and be crowned champion of the world.

The teams lined up for the race. *(Pause)* January coughed in anticipation. *(Pause)* February scratched its head while it waited. *(Pause)* March tried to get in a quick snooze. *(Pause)* April went to find a hot dog vendor. *(Pause)* May jogged in place. *(Pause)* June practiced bowing for the victory celebration. *(Pause)* July combed its hair. *(Pause)* August put sunscreen on its face and hands. *(Pause)* September tried to catch up on homework. *(Pause)* October sang "Mary Had a Little Lamb" to overcome its nervousness. *(Pause)* November's allergies made it sneeze. *(Pause)* And December made out its Christmas list. *(Pause)*

Suddenly a shot rang out, and the race began. The first leg of the race was underwater bicycling. One by one, team members mounted their bikes and rode into the lake. *(Pause)* They tried to go as fast as they could, but the water resistance made it look like they were moving in slow motion. *(Pause)*

Round and round the lake they rode, *(Pause)* until July and February wrecked, which in turn caused December and April to lose their balance. *(Pause)* All four teams lay in a jumbled mess in the middle of the shallow lake, *(Pause)* and the race had to be momentarily stopped. *(Pause)*

During the break, an enterprising spectator shouted, "Hey, why don't we have a pep rally?" So they did. One by one, the teams took turns performing cheers. *(Pause)* When all teams were done, everyone at the race responded with a full 15-second standing ovation. *(Pause)*

The judges decided the contestants should move on to the next portion of the race. So after everyone parked and dismounted their bicycles, *(Pause)* the teams jogged to the train station. *(Pause)*

At the station, the judges informed contestants they were to create a human train and chug around the racetrack in synchronized motions. Points would be awarded for style, efficiency, and originality. Without hesitation, the teams rushed to perform. *(Pause)*

Everything seemed to be going swimmingly, until January, March, June, and September forgot to look where they were going and chugged right onto hot sand. Their trains broke formation, and they danced about trying to get off the burning sand. *(Pause)* The rest of the teams laughed until they cried. *(Pause)*

So the judges directed everyone to the third portion of the race—the talent competition. The judges gave teams two minutes to work up imitations of their favorite musical groups. Then each team performed for the others. *(Pause)* After all were done, the applause was deafening. *(Pause)* Everyone took a bow. *(Pause)* But no one was sure exactly who was winning.

May, August, and November were starting to tire. *(Pause)* One by one, each team collapsed onto the floor. *(Pause)* They'd given up. For the rest of the race May, August, and November would be spectators.

The other nine teams got ready for the fourth portion of the race—the helicopter relay. They lined up for the relay—one in which each team member ran from one side of the stadium to the other, twirling in circles and fanning his or her arms overhead. The gun sounded, and the relay began. *(Pause)* The three teams who had dropped out earlier cheered wildly for the competing teams. *(Pause)*

When it was over, March, April, and June were so dizzy they all passed out. *(Pause)* That left only six teams to compete in the final portion of the contest—drag racing.

Just as the race was about to begin, February, July, and September started having doubts and walked around in circles curiously tapping their heads. *(Pause)* A spectator said, "Face facts, February, July, and September. You just don't have what it takes to win. Drop out now before you embarrass yourselves." Discouraged, they joined the other teams on the sidelines. *(Pause)*

January, October, and December climbed into their drag racing cars, revved their engines, *(Pause)* and honked their horns.

(Pause) The race began, and January, October, and December sped around the track. *(Pause)* When it was over, the judges couldn't pick a clear winner, so they awarded all three teams first prize. January, October, and December did jumping jacks in their joy of being crowned champions of the world. *(Pause)*

Then they noticed the nine teams who had dropped out of the race. *(Pause)* January, October, and December were so happy at having won, they invited the other teams to a victory party. *(Pause)*

And everyone laughed happily as they went to eat the fantastic snacks a local church had provided for all the contestants in ... the Super Race!

BEFORE THE FINAL CURTAIN

Have kids read Philippians 3:12-14 and discuss these questions.
1. How did you feel during this skit? Explain. How was the Super Race like our daily Christian life?
2. During the skit, why did teams give up on their goals of winning the race? Why do people give up on their dreams and goals in life? How can Philippians 3:12-14 help us as we strive to achieve our goals?
3. How do your dreams and goals compare to God's dreams for you? How can God help us choose wise goals to pursue? What is one goal you have for your Christian life?

AFTER THE SHOW

Try these activities for further study.
1. Take the youth group to a professional or amateur sporting event. Have kids all sit together and cheer for both teams. After the game (and a few hot dogs!), discuss how the winning and losing teams might feel. Help kids explore what the losing team can do to overcome its failure to achieve its goal of winning. Compare that to what kids can do when they fall short in life.
2. Have a goal-setting party. At the party, give kids paper and pencils and encourage them to set the following goals:
    - a one-, five-, and 10-year goal for their personal lives;
    - a one-, five-, and 10-year goal for their academic lives;
    - a one-, five-, and 10-year goal for their spiritual lives; and
    - a lifetime goal to somehow change the world for the better.

Tell kids to take their goals home, keep them in a safe place, and refer to them often. Close with a prayer that God will help group members achieve honorable and satisfying goals.

MORE CREATIVE PROGRAMMING IDEAS FROM

60-SECOND SKITS

by Chuck Bolte and Paul McCusker

Trigger faith-building discussions in your group—and help kids apply God's Word to their daily lives—with these quick and easy skits. You'll unlock teenagers' feelings about...

- love
- popularity
- the environment
- conflict
- cheating
- friendship
- suicide
- outreach
- caring
- pregnancy
- parents
- divorce

... plus, dating... evangelism... forgiveness... and loads of other issues facing today's young people. Each skit is followed by thought-provoking questions to get kids talking and handy scripture references to help young people discover biblical answers.

Youth workers will spend less time planning meetings—and bring kids closer to God—with these no-preparation, few-or-no-props-needed skits!

ISBN 1-55945-036-3

QUICK CROWDBREAKERS AND GAMES FOR YOUTH GROUPS

Over 200 sure-fire icebreakers guaranteed to get meetings, retreats, and lock-ins off to a lively start... ready in an instant! Taken from "Try This One," a popular section in GROUP Magazine, you'll choose from...

- Pair Games—like Blind Prince Shoe Grab, Cotton Ball Catch, Ice Cream Special, Looks Like Rain
- Team Tangles—like Autograph Round-Up, Jousters, Marshmallow Drop, Name That Hymn, Newspaper Crumple
- Just for Fun activities—like Church Clues, Close-Up Sounds, Hum That Tune, Laugh Machine, Marching Kazoos

... and much more. These are creative games perfect for whenever kids get together.

ISBN 0-931529-46-8

Available at your local Christian bookstore. Or write:
Group Publishing, Inc., Box 485, Loveland, CO 80539.